I0418357

REWRITTEN

Rewritten

AN ADULTERESS REDEEMED

Laura Ramchand Villena

Atlanta, GA
www.Pinpoint.pub

Copyright © 2024 by Laura Villena

All rights reserved

No portion of this book may be reproduced, stored in a retrieval system, or transmitted in any form by any means–electronic, mechanical, photocopy, recording, or other–except for brief quotations in printed reviews, without prior permission of the author.

Unless stated otherwise, Scripture quotations are taken from the HOLY BIBLE, NEW INTERNATIONAL VERSION. Copyright © 1973, 1978, 1984 by International Bible Society. Used by permission of Hodder & Stoughton Publishers, a member of the Hachette UK Group. All rights reserved. 'NIV' is a registered trademark of the International Bible Society. UK trademark number 1448790.

Scripture quotations marked "Amplified" are taken from the AmplifiedBible (AMP), Copyright © 2015 by The Lockman Foundation. Used by permission. www.Lockman.org

Paperback ISBN: 979-8-89786-000-5

eBook ISBN: 979-8-89786-001-2

Thank you to my husband, Jose Villena.
Thank you for your permission to share my account of our story.
Thank you for believing *with* me that our story can ignite hope for others and that our restoration experience can increase faith in others. You keep me always moving forward. This story exists because of you.

A great big thank you to my dad, Reynold W. Ramchand.
Thank you for playing a major part in my restoration story. Thank you for loving and supporting me at every turn, even when you disagreed with my choices. You made the way forward possible for me however you could. I have always been your princess and you made sure I'd never forget that. I love you always, Dad.
Til I see you again…

Forward

"REWRITTEN, An Adulteress Redeemed" is not just a title; it is a profound declaration of hope, a testament to the Father's transformative power of grace and mercy. This book narrates the journey of Laura Villena, a woman whose life story encapsulates the essence of falling and rising, of losing and finding, of sin and redemption.

Laura's story is a stark reminder of our human frailties. Her journey into the depths of adultery and the consequent shattering of a family is a poignant reflection of the choices we make and their far-reaching consequences. It speaks to the heart of every person who has ever stumbled, who has ever felt the heavy burden of guilt and the pain of being lost.

Yet, what makes Laura's story remarkable is not just her fall but her rise. It is a narrative of how she found her way back to the Lord, a journey marked by introspection, repentance, and an unwavering pursuit of redemption. Laura's story is a powerful illustration of the truth that no matter how far we stray, the path back to grace is always open.

This book dives deep into the very heart of what it means to be redeemed. It speaks of a grace that doesn't just forgive but restores, a mercy that doesn't merely erase the past but rewrites it. Laura's life is a living testament to the fact that our worst moments do not define us; instead, it is our willingness to turn back, to change, and to accept the grace that is offered to us that shapes our true identity.

In these pages, you will find not just the story of Laura Villena but also an invitation to reflect on your own life. Her journey encourages us to look beyond our faults and failures and to see ourselves as more than the sum of our mistakes. It is an inspiration to embrace the grace and mercy of God, which are powerful enough to transform our lives, rewrite our stories, and offer us a second chance.

As you embark on this journey with Laura, may you be inspired to believe in the power of redemption. May her story remind you that no one is beyond the reach of God's grace and that every life, no matter how broken, can be rewritten into a beautiful testament of divine love and mercy.

Pastor Manny Rivera

CONTENTS

INTRODUCTION

For the first thirty years of my life, I worked hard to live a life worthy of writing down, one day, an inspirational life story. I just knew, even from an early age, that humanity would eventually benefit from knowing my life's story. I was going to be an actress or maybe a news anchor; maybe I could do one and then the other. Sometimes I included God in the details, but due to some hurtful interactions I'd had with Christians and the church, I mostly tried to do things on my own. I was constantly seeking things like comfort, security, and peace from the people in my life, but they could never fulfill what I needed. Eventually, after a ten-year hiatus from church and anything to do with faith or Christianity, I realized that only Jesus could fulfill what I'd been seeking from other people. I'd experienced God before, but a decade of pain had made a chasm in my heart where I'd separated myself from the things of God.

I thought that I could control how my story would go, maybe not every detail, but certainly the ending. I kept journals chronicling what was happening both for my review and so I could retell every detail for the myriads of people that would be hanging on my every word. I never imagined writing the story I'm writing today but that's the truly amazing part of it all. God has had more in mind than my fame or success, more than achieving my version of the American Dream. My story, rewritten by His hand and for His glory, is bigger than just another small-town kid who made something of herself.

Over the last seven years, I've been growing in my relationship with God and now I'm watching as God rewrites my story and redeems my past for His glory. I'm finding everything in Him that I could not find in other people. He has taken my loneliness, despair, pain, and heartbreak and has restored me through His presence, comfort, and peace.

Over the years, as people met me and my family, and saw the way we lived together as a blended family, they were curious. Most families remain tense after divorce. Ex-spouses rarely get along, and stepfamilies often come with a lifetime of unresolved wounds. But our story was different—different than what people expected, different than what seemed possible.

Again and again, people asked how? How did we go from brokenness, betrayal, and bitterness to redemption, restoration, and peace? How could something so shattered be made whole?

The answer was never *us*. It was never our ability, our wisdom, or our effort. The answer was, and will always be, **Jesus**.

When I would explain the miracle He had worked in our lives, the response was always the same: *You have to write this down.* People need to hear this.

So here it is. This is our story, but more importantly, this is God's story—proof of what happens when we submit to His will, His design, and His ability to rewrite even the worst of our mistakes. My prayer is that through these pages, you find hope. That no matter what you've done, what you've lost, or how far you think you've fallen, you will see what restoration can look like. Because if He can do it for us, He can do it for you.

My aim in writing this book is to share with you what I walked through so that you are encouraged to walk out your journey and so you can rejoice in your redemption. I want to give you hope! Living life according to my own rules and making myself happy only made an enormous mess. I am willing to share with you my mistakes, my regrets, and truly the worst parts of myself so that you see the amazing change a life can experience when given over to Jesus. There's a quote I love that says, "One day, you will tell your story of how you've overcome what you're going through now, and it will become a part of someone else's survival guide." When you hand the pen over to God, you'll be amazed at all He has in store for you. Life, according to His design, is better than anything you could ask for or imagine.

Part One
THE AUTHOR OF
MY OWN STORY

1

SEEKING APPROVAL

My mother raised me in church for as long as I can remember. I loved the people who were happy to see me every week and greeted me with a hug and a smile. I loved the songs and the stories about God. I learned very well the difference between right and wrong and how to be a good person. In my teenage years, I knew how to look the part, but I had a very shallow understanding and an equally shallow relationship with God. I knew all the right answers but I was doing Christianity my way. Like many immature believers, I struggled with doing what God wanted versus what I wanted. For a while there, I attempted to do both. When I was about sixteen years old, a prophet at my church told me, "Things would go so much better for you when you learn to live one life and be of one mind." I can still see him merging his hands palm to palm.

By my junior year of high school, I'd developed a distaste for the emptiness of drinking and smoking to be cool and using promiscuity to try to fill the void in my heart. I knew I needed to make a change, to rededicate myself to the things of God. I was determined to follow the rules to be that good person I'd learned about in my childhood. I heard about a discipleship program in Georgia and felt like this was my new lease on life. My mom and I planned a trip to visit the campus and it was incredible! I met other young adults who not only had fun together but were passionate about serving God and knowing Him intimately. I had never heard adults pray like they did, much less people near my age! They were more than classmates, something closer to a family and I wanted desperately to be a part of it. Over the following year, I was convinced there was nowhere else for me. In all honesty, I was afraid to try for college and didn't know what I would study if I dared to apply. I considered one art school in New York but I had so little confidence in myself to make good choices, much less succeed at chasing a dream! I applied to the discipleship program and was accepted. It felt good to have a plan and I was excited to be a part of the passion I'd seen on my visit the year prior. My mom and I figured out the tuition and when I graduated high school, I moved to Georgia. What I didn't know was that in the year between my visit and the beginning of the program, the leadership had changed. Instead of the seasoned leaders who had been there for some years, two newlywed graduates of the program had been put in place as directors. They were not much older than the students in the program but they led to the best of their ability. Unfortunately, as young leaders, mistakes were made.

Please understand as I share this part of my story with you that I have already forgiven these leaders and experienced a great deal of maturity, discipline, and healing. I take full responsibility for the part I played in the poor communication, my lack of accountability, and my rebellion. I hadn't known the kind of discipleship relationship that I was introduced to and expected to participate in. I didn't understand what it meant or how to follow a leader in that type of mentorship. I have to explain what I felt and believed to be true at that time to properly explain the wounds I experienced, even if they were self-inflicted. You must understand that our enemy does not care about immaturity. He doesn't take it easy on us because the people around us are doing their best, and one day, we'll understand. Our enemy is ruthless, conniving, and a liar, and when we believe his lies, we allow ourselves to be hurt, and our perspective gets twisted. My leaders did not intentionally hurt me, and yet I was very hurt by what happened.

SELF-RELIANCE AND THE DOWNWARD SPIRAL

I was seventeen years old, running away from my behavior, and determined to do the right thing from here on out. I was capable of making the right choices, I just hadn't always chosen them in my hometown. I knew that if I focused, if I removed myself from tempting situations if I dove head first into what God wanted me to do, then I wouldn't have time to sin anymore. (Did you catch that? I, I, I...) The students around me were from different parts of the country, some even from other countries! We got to know each other and made pledges to look out for each other. We became family. We celebrated holidays together and told each other our stories. I saw my classmates get close to our leaders, and have approving words spoken over them. As much as I craved it, for some reason, I didn't feel the same acceptance from our leaders. I was careful how much I shared with them because I wanted them to like me. I tried so hard to do everything they asked but it didn't seem to matter. I felt, especially from the female leader, that there was more she wanted from me than I could give. It seemed to me that she preferred the other girls over me, and nothing I could do or say would change that. I was frustrated, feeling denied, and overlooked left and right. I couldn't understand how the incredible things about God I was learning and experiencing could be nearly opposite to what I experienced from my leaders, who served and pursued the same God. I was told that I was too loud and drew too much attention to myself. I was told that I was manipulative and wanted to control those around me, especially the boys. I was told that I was using my parents' divorce and the trauma that followed as an excuse for my bad behavior. Frustrated and angry, I went back to what I knew would provide me some relief. I acted out and "made out" with one of the boys in my class. Truth be told, I did want to feel more in control of my life. Promiscuity was easy and a guaranteed, expected response, with no surprises and no disappointments. Self-loathing, yes, but more importantly to me at the time was the assured, although sick, kind of comfort that promiscuity would bring. This young man was just a pawn to me; there was no honor in my actions, regardless of how far we did or didn't go. The details didn't matter to justify anything; my heart was in such a gross place, and only wounding could come out of it. Afterwards, he quickly and voluntarily confessed to our leaders what we had done but I had to be called in for a meeting. Of course, I had no desire to confess to my leaders when I made mistakes because I was sure those mistakes would be used as ammunition against me. Trying to do everything for my leaders' approval was exhausting and impossible and left the same void I'd been living with before my move to Georgia. In so many ways, the void felt worse. I told myself that since I could not do the right thing in their eyes anyway, I'd do what at least made me feel good for a moment. And it was just a moment. Although I couldn't see it, my life, more than ever before, was the perfect reflection of Galatians 1:10:

10 *Am I now trying to win the approval of human beings, or God?*
Or am I trying to please people? If I were still trying to please peo-
ple, I would not be a servant of Christ.

SELF-FOCUS AND DESPAIR

My leaders were very disappointed in me, with good reason.
My punishment was to translate all of the books of Proverbs into
my own words and write a report on two Christian-authored books
describing the dangers of dating. I was to stay by myself in the
dorm until it was completed. After I turned in the work, I had a
follow-up meeting with the female leader of the discipleship program and another female leader at the church whom I didn't know
well. The purpose of the meeting was to determine my level of
repentance and, based on that, my worthiness to continue in the
program. They opened the meeting by warning me about the spirit
of Jezebel that I carried. I don't remember much more of what they
said after that. I felt so defeated. They still didn't trust me even
though I'd done the punishment I'd been assigned. They didn't
seem to hear what I had to say and weren't interested in the good
things I'd learned. Not even how translating Proverbs had become
fun and exciting. The Bible came alive to me for the first time and
I was grateful for the time and the assignment despite it being a
punishment. Perhaps despite their better judgment, I was allowed
to stay and finish the second year of the discipleship program.

A few months later, on an overseas mission trip, we had our
end-of-term interviews. The discipleship program was designed to
last for two years with the possibility of a third year as a leader by
invitation only. After that, most graduates found a place on staff or
in leadership at the church. I had many questions still, but the safe-

ty of the bubble around this community was so appealing to me. I wanted to stay connected to these people, to Jesus, and I believed that safety and Jesus only existed here in this bubble. I'm sure it's no surprise to you that in my end-of-term interview, I was not invited back for the third year, but somehow, I was shocked, and it hit me very hard. I felt so rejected. I felt like they'd just turned me loose as a lost cause, a write-off. I didn't want to go back to my hometown; I knew what was waiting for me there, and I didn't want that life. I knew exactly who I could call if I went home, the people I would fall back in company with, and probably the man I would have ended up married to. In the days following my exit interview, I felt like I was staring down the barrel of the inevitable, but I refused to give up and settle for that life. I had very little hope for the future except to hold on as best as I could to a better version of myself. I'd put all my effort into pleasing people and gaining their approval, keeping my eyes off of God and His love and grace for me. I was ultimately left unfulfilled because it wasn't God I was trying to please. I would have said then that I was trying my best to follow Christ, but the community I was in didn't feel like a community; I felt isolated and misunderstood.

The discipleship program was connected to a prominent church in the Atlanta area, and the junior high youth pastor and his wife invited me to live with their family. I would be able to stay in Georgia and stay involved at the church at least. This couple had invited other students to live with them in the past and I was excited to stay and keep learning. What I didn't know was that this couple had been having marriage problems, and my arrival into that environment created the perfect storm.

2

SEEKING
COMFORT

I began my time living with Jose, his wife, and their four children in August of 2005. Jose had been mentored by the same leader who had formerly led the discipleship program. Together they had built and led the youth ministry into a powerful revival. Jose knew about the Bible and God. His wife was pretty quiet and kept to herself, but she seemed nice enough, and she and Jose had agreed to take me in to live with them after my time in the discipleship program ended. I was so grateful to be able to stay in Georgia and keep attending the church.

The youth and young adult ministries of the church had a lot of the same passion that had initially attracted me to move to Georgia to begin with. I made a few friends, but I tended to keep them at arm's length because I didn't want to taint them since I was such a failure and still so full of wickedness. I had a very hard time understanding why the season of my life in the discipleship program had been so hard. Based on what I knew then, I could only conclude that what my leaders had said about my seeking control over others, seeking any opportunity to manipulate, must be true and I should consider myself lucky to be allowed to stay in the vicinity of such holy people. I kept my head down and tried to stay out of trouble.

Jose took notice and pushed me to be honest about what I was feeling. He was so helpful and comforting, accepting me no matter what I said. Jose was the first person to make me feel like a human who had made mistakes rather than a gross, dirty thing that was a mistake. Jose and I would engage in lots of deep, intimate conversations alone, just the two of us. He would ask how I was feeling or otherwise start the conversation while his wife was still in the room, but after an hour or so, she would leave, and it would be just Jose and me. Both of us knew that was not the right way to go about it, but I couldn't let go of how normal and okay Jose made me feel. No one else could understand what I was thinking and feeling the way he did and still serve God. Most people who had seen or experienced the negative parts of my character either encouraged the negative behavior or got scared off. I pushed many people away, rejecting them before they could reject me. In Jose, I found a safe harbor, someone who saw good in me. I don't recall him ever telling me to find my answers in Jesus. I remember Jose was an open door; if I ever wanted to talk, I could always go to him. He encouraged me to keep going to church and surrounding myself with good things so that good would win. He also told me not to be so hard on myself and that there were worse people than me in the world. Of course, I clung to him. Jose became the answer to everything that I felt was missing. It was his voice that filled the void in my heart and drowned out all the negative voices. I wanted to reciprocate, to give him something in exchange for the life and hope he had spoken over me.

Since I was clinging to Jose and his words, chasing good and not God, I still carried all the sickness of perspective I'd brought with me from childhood. Holy Spirit is described as The Comforter. The design of God is to find comfort in Him, not in another person. He has to be the answer for the missing pieces in our hearts so that what fills our hearts is perfect and without end. Even the healthiest relationships with people will encounter problems. The best people are still imperfect. Only Jesus can be everything we need. As He makes us whole, we can then be the best in our relationships with others and we will know to point them to Jesus and not ourselves. Scripturally that principle is found in 2 Corinthians 1:3-5:

3 Blessed be the God and Father of our Lord Jesus Christ, the Father of mercies and God of all comfort, 4 who comforts us in all our affliction, so that we may be able to comfort those who are in any affliction, with the comfort with which we ourselves are comforted by God. 5 For as we share abundantly in Christ's sufferings, so through Christ we share abundantly in comfort too.

RIPPLES START SMALL, BUT THEY GROW

In Chapter 1, I alluded to my parents' divorce and the trauma I experienced at six years of age. When we experience trauma, especially at a young age, we can take lessons away from it that are twisted and false because of our limited understanding. Then, even as adults who can now rationalize the situation with compassion for those involved, we tend to operate on the understanding of life we formed as children. It's as if our brain is an operating system whose code is being written as we experience life. Later in life, the operating system is still executing code that was written during immaturity and ignorance. What I took away from my life experience when I was six, which no one ever said to me, ran so deeply and true in my heart that thirteen years later, as a young adult, I was making decisions rooted in this twisted perspective. I believed a woman needed to be, first and foremost, a sexual creature. If she wasn't, then she had nothing of value to give to those around her. If sex were not part of the relationship, then the woman would be abandoned and left alone.

Everything feels so big and so final as a teenager. Reality can be hard to find in the absence of wise counsel. Jose was the only one I was confiding in and I was being rewarded with acceptance. Life's circumstances required Jose and his family to move forty-five minutes away from the church we were all involved in. I had the opportunity to move in with other friends but instead, I wanted to stay with Jose. We both worked in the same area, about an hour's commute, so to save on gas, we rode to and from work together. We talked about everything and Jose would say it was the first time he felt really listened to. He was allowed to tell me any story and it was met with interest and acceptance, not dismissal or judgment. I was filling gaps in him as well that I had no business filling. It wasn't too long before mutual, unconditional acceptance turned into something else: an unhealthy, mutual, emotional connection followed by a sexual affair. I didn't know any other way to express gratitude for the depth of admiration I was feeling. Sex was the pinnacle of what all guys wanted, right? That's what a woman does to love, appreciate, and give to the men in her life, right? Sex is what keeps a man around, right?

There was a particular winter when Jose and his wife had a horrible, public fight in which Jose found his excuse to leave her.

He told me he was done trying to make it work with his wife. She had expressed in this fight that there was no way he could make her happy. It was the open door we had both been waiting for. The commute made everything possible. We found reasons to stay late in the city before making the hour's drive back home to his wife and family. My life became so splintered, no longer split in two but however many pieces it took to keep going. My friends wondered why I stayed so far away. My coworkers wondered why I smiled to myself sometimes. Everyone wondered why I kept so much to myself instead of going out with friends. I wondered how long I could keep up with all the lies and excuses. One thing was for sure: nothing made sense.

It's like Paul says in Romans 7:15-20:

15 I do not understand what I do. For what I want to do I do not do, but what I hate I do. 16 And if I do what I do not want to do, I agree that the law is good. 17 As it is, it is no longer I myself who do it, but it is sin living in me. 18 For I know that good itself does not dwell in me, that is, in my sinful nature.[a] For I have the desire to do what is good, but I cannot carry it out. 19 For I do not do the good I want to do, but the evil I do not want to do—this I keep on doing. 20 Now if I do what I do not want to do, it is no longer I who do it, but it is sin living in me that does it.

CAUSE AND EFFECT

I knew better than to say yes to promiscuity again. I knew better than to say yes to an affair. My own parents' divorce was due to infidelity. Still, I carried on playing pretend with Jose. He told me he could breathe around me. I told him everything about me and he didn't run away. We used each other to soothe our wounds without considering how we were wounding the people around us. I'd like to say we came to our senses on our own, but instead, we were caught on a date by one of his family members. It was only then that the rose-colored glasses and the excuses I'd made for myself all came crashing down. I couldn't believe what I'd done and I felt sick about it. Truth be told, I had been feeling sick for a few weeks at this point but guilt tends to do that to a person. I quickly planned to move home to live with my brother and his family while I got my head back on straight. One Sunday before I was due to leave town, I felt too sick to go to church, so instead, I went to see a movie. No sooner had the lights gone down, and the movie started when I got a phone call. The senior youth pastor who served as Jose's leader was on the line, and he wanted me to come in for a meeting. I had no history or relationship with this pastor but he was not letting me off the hook. I left the theater and headed to the church building. We met in his office, just the youth pastor and I. I was petrified. He told me he knew what had happened between Jose and me because Jose had confessed and stepped down as junior high youth pastor. He knew I had trouble during my time in the discipleship program as well, specifically in not confessing when I'd made a mistake with sexual misconduct. He told me I'd done enough damage and needed to disappear so that Jose and his wife could reconcile and so that no one else at the church was taken advantage of by me. The room spun. I don't know how I responded, except that I fled as fast as I could, and I was not going to cry in front of this guy. What did he know about me anyway? We had literally never spoken before! I was planning to leave anyway, so his advice worked for me. I did disappear to my hometown within the week, but not before I'd spoken to my brother again about the whole situation and confirmed I could stay with him. I'm very close to my brother, so when I told him about the affair and how

I'd been feeling sick, he asked me about my cycle and if everything was normal there. He was a father himself and understood basic biology, so he recognized the signs I was ignoring. Very calmly, he suggested I take a pregnancy test, just in case. On my lunch break from work, in a Target bathroom stall, I took one test... The positive result popped up unbelievably fast. I took a second test shortly after I returned to work that day with the same very quick, very boldly positive result. As I drove north up the interstate to my brother's house, I had a very quick phone call with Jose. It felt like the right thing to do to let him know I was going home and also that I was pregnant and the baby was his. I was washing my hands of this whole mess, imagining that he would figure out his marriage and I would figure out how to be a mom on my own. I found out later that Jose was with his wife in Colorado on a "goodbye" trip and he was at that moment in an interview with a prominent pastor to turn down a job offer in person. He planned to pursue a relationship with me but he wasn't sure what that looked like. I couldn't think about what that looked like either or if I even wanted it but I was not waiting around — I was going home.

At the beginning of the affair, conviction pressed at me, but I *fought* it. I shoved it aside, buried it under layers of resentment and bitterness. I felt rejected by God. When I wasn't invited to stay a part of the ministry school, it felt like a door had been slammed shut on me—like God's people had cast me out. So, in my mind, I wasn't walking into sin—I was *getting even*.

I told myself I didn't care. That doing the right thing had gotten me nowhere, so I might as well do the wrong thing and enjoy it. Of course, I didn't enjoy it. Not really.

As conviction continued, it twisted itself into something even darker—**shame**. I wasn't just *doing* bad things; I was a *bad* person. I was proving them right—the ones who had dismissed me, who had looked at me with judgment and disappointment. I must be exactly what they thought. And if that was the case, why even try?

So I leaned in further.

Eventually, I was diagnosed with depression—not because of the affair itself, but because I had completely swallowed the belief that I was *beyond redemption*.

But that was a lie. And I wouldn't fully grasp that truth until the day I finally stopped **running from conviction** and started **running toward God**.

3

SEEKING A HOPEFUL FUTURE

I had left my small hometown in 2003, so confident that I would never return. Life held more for me than what I could find in North Carolina. I needed more space, more air to breathe — adventure! My heart at seventeen was so proud of itself and full of pity for my friends who were left behind. I burned all the bridges on my way to bigger and better things. Now, three short years later, I was returning with my tail between my legs. I'd failed epically. The adventure I found myself in was not at all what I had hoped for. It was all a huge mess. Despite my chagrin, my family welcomed me with open arms. Their response to me returning home with a surprise pregnancy was more positive than I'd expected, and it was a relief to find a safe harbor. My brother and nephew were happy to see me and have me stay with them. They offered no judgment, and they were excited as my pregnancy progressed. My mother knew before I confessed to her why I'd come home. She assured me that God had already prepared her for my news and that while I had messed up, it was time to focus on staying healthy and celebrating the baby. My father said he would have preferred Jose, and I waited. If his marriage was truly failing, we should have done things in the right order. He said our hormones got the better of us, and so they had, but he was supportive as well.

Jose followed up with me via email and phone calls, promising to visit me. He would tell me how much he missed me and all the things he wanted for us moving forward. It was beautiful stuff to hear, but deep down, I didn't actually believe him. No one ever pursued me —- no one ever had to. Once, I had spent time with a guy, and things had gotten hot and heavy, as they usually did; the guy always seemed to move on to another girl. Except for maybe one or two relationships I had in high school, I was not someone taken seriously, someone cherished. When I was, I didn't trust or appreciate it and so I sabotaged it. To my surprise, while I hid in the safety of my hometown for several months, Jose came to visit me twice, although not without incident.

His dream was to have me and all of his children together but he was hesitant on how to make that happen. The fear was always that because he was the one who committed infidelity if his wife ever decided to file for divorce, then she would easily win custody of the kids. In juggling that fear and trying to determine what he wanted next, Jose would give me one explanation and tell his wife something totally different. I found out that Jose was still living with his wife and sleeping with her, but he assured me it was just because he didn't want to lose his kids. What could I say to that? How could I be indignant and demand he stop sleeping with his wife? How could I demand that he just leave her and his kids? I was the mistress, I was the villain and in no place to demand anything. In my history, my dad lived next door after my parents divorced, and I loved having both my parents in my life every day, so I fully supported Jose's wanting to keep his kids close. I did tell Jose that he didn't have to stay with me. He could keep his wife and kids and still see our baby. I wouldn't keep it from him whether he and I were together or not. Again he would tell me that was not what he wanted — he just needed time.

I was focused on the baby more than on my relationship status, but I did love Jose. The idea was new and scary and fragile but I wanted to believe in the picture Jose would paint for me. No one had ever known me as completely as he did, and certainly, no one else wanted to know me that exhaustively. I had no idea what being a stepmom would be like, but I did love his kids. At twenty years of age, I honestly believed we would just figure it out. I was convinced and decided to trust him and make a go of it. Let's just see where it would take us.

IGNORING THE TRUTH

Around five or six months along in my pregnancy, I agreed to visit Jose back in Georgia. There had been some drama around his trips to see me, and planning around time with the kids would be easier if he was still in town rather than out of state. Unexpectedly, I spent the majority of the time alone in a hotel, cycling between confusion, fear, and anger. Every time I was ready to leave and go back home, I'd get a text, and I'd wait a little longer. Jose did make it there eventually and told me some story about how he was stuck and trying to get to me all day. I found out after we had slept together that Jose's wife had found out I was in town, and so to avoid more arguing, Jose decided I could wait. He said spent the day at the park with his wife and kids. I was furious and reeling. Was I making a mistake? Was it too late for me now? Who else would want me anyway? I continued to tell Jose that I would be fine on my own and that he didn't have to string me along but I never ended it. When he would reassure me, I chose to believe it. I wanted to believe it. It was so much easier to make Jose's wife the villain and blame her for "our troubles" than to do the responsible and right thing. I clung to my hope that it would somehow all turn out — I clung to my desire for Jose and my selfishness to keep him.

Before returning to North Carolina, an old classmate from the discipleship program contacted me to say she wanted to see me and invited me to meet her at our old church. To my surprise, I ended up sitting with her and our former leader for yet another meeting. He asked me about repentance and my plans, none of which I knew for sure. Repentance, as I recall he explained it, was cutting Jose out of my life completely. Even after a horrible and sad visit, since he was my baby's father, that wasn't something I was comfortable promising. This was not the answer my former leader was hoping to hear. He went on to say that in my refusal to repent, I was cursing my daughter to repeat my mistakes. I was foolish to hang on to him in any way and should expect Jose to one day cheat on me as he had cheated on his wife. My friend just sat there and cried. How dare she! I was the one who had been tricked into a meeting just to be attacked. Nothing my former leader said made sense to me or aligned with what I understood about God. Nothing he said now seemed to match what he had taught us during the discipleship program.

As mentioned previously, I retell this story from my perspective as it was then, as a hard-headed adulteress consumed in my sin. I now understand the biblical truth that this leader was trying to express to me, but at the time I received his counsel as if he had expressed it with no love and no hope. In 1 Corinthians 5, Paul instructs the church on how to deal with unrepentant believers who commit sexually immoral sin. Jose and I both refused to follow the biblical process of repentance that was offered to us at the time because we liked our sin too much and made excuses for it. It felt cruel to send Jose back to a wife who didn't want him. It felt unfair to deny my unborn child the presence of her father and we saw no reason why he couldn't have all his kids together. There was no understanding or willingness to restore the covenant marriage relationship Jose had broken with his wife. Our former leaders were not ogres —- they were not mean, spiteful, or cruel. They were biblically obedient and they handed us over to Satan. It was painful and confusing for them and us.

Several covenant relationships had been ripped apart and yet Jose and I remained rebellious and incredibly selfish, accepting heartily the bait of the enemy for us to shift blame and play the victims. We were determined to stay in our sin no matter the cost. We were arrogant to think it was a price we would be willing or even able to pay. I wish I could say this was the dumbest that we got, but sadly, we had just begun to dive head-first into the pig pen. It would be more than a decade of foolishness and before we "came to ourselves" like the prodigal son in the Gospel of Luke, chapter fifteen. Our lives were a true reflection of Romans 1:28:

28 Furthermore, just as they did not think it worthwhile to retain the knowledge of God, so God gave them over to a depraved mind, so that they do what ought not to be done.

HARDENING OF HEART

I'm unsure how I got back home from the meeting with my leader that day. The list of people who'd promised to be by my side was vanishing. I had my mom, dad, and brother. I might have had

Jose. Things were hard to process, especially due to my refusal to see reason and do the obvious, right thing, but I had more than myself to think about. I couldn't wallow in confusion or wrestle with indecision any longer. It was time to settle on a path and get to walking. I pulled on my big girl britches and pressed into what I thought was best. I didn't want to raise my daughter away from her father, who wanted her. I didn't want to push away the man who understood me and wanted me. I was not interested in dating someone else —- I wanted Jose. We decided I would move to Georgia to live with Jose, to give birth there, and to be us against the world. We wanted to be together with *all* of Jose's kids and I signed up to help work toward that goal. We comforted ourselves by saying that an epic love story was fraught with troubles that had to be overcome.

Despite the way I got there and the drama along the way, I absolutely loved being pregnant. I did not have to deal with much sickness or side effects. I put on a good amount of weight, but I'd never filled out a pair of jeans so well, and I loved that. I bonded with my daughter over those beautiful nine months carrying her and reassured her that she was wanted and would be loved, that she was already loved. I would rub my belly and apologize to her often for the stress that maybe she was picking up on from me. I would sing what lyrics I could remember of Dumbo's "Baby Mine" to her. I couldn't wait to hold her and stare at her, count her fingers and toes, and smell her baby smell. I wasn't sure of anything else but I was sure I was going to be a good mom. I would protect her fiercely and she would have everything she needed and everything I could give of what she wanted.

My family remained supportive while I was in North Carolina, always reminding me that the baby was a blessing. They helped me get excited about being a mom and celebrate the life growing inside me. They did not understand what was happening with Jose and me, whether we were going to end up together or even if we should. My brother was my biggest confidant, and his advice was mainly to do what I thought was best for "me and the kid." I went back to work at a custard shop I'd worked at one summer in high school. My old manager hired me, understanding I'd have to leave within a few months. I went to my doctor's appointments with my mom and I kept Jose posted on how things were going. We celebrated finding out I was having a daughter, and we researched names together online. He would always say he wanted the baby to have his name and to be born in Georgia. I was about seven-and-a-half months along when Jose and I had the conversation that I couldn't make the six-hour drive each way to visit him any longer. If he really wanted me and the baby there, then I should move in now. He agreed. Even after experiencing how messy it would be for us to try to be together in Georgia, I loaded up my few belongings and drove my manual transmission truck down to stay with Jose at his apartment and hope for the best. My mom came with me but drove separately so that she could help me get set up before returning home.

We had a nice weekend together, and then, on Monday, Jose went to work, my mom went home to North Carolina, and I stayed at the apartment I would now share with Jose. Something, however, must have gotten lost in the communication. Despite all the conversations, despite discussing that I was too far along in my pregnancy to drive back and forth, despite my mom driving separately and my having a lot of stuff with me in my truck —- Jose did not realize I was moving in that weekend. We laugh about it now, but Jose was surprised to find me still there on Monday evening when he came home from work. I cannot imagine the mental load he was carrying for it not to click. Even now, he can't explain why he didn't put the two together, but he will say that he is glad I pushed to be there when I did. I'm sure as you read this, you're screaming for me to run, to see the truth and get out, but don't worry. It does get better —- but not yet. Proverbs 3:5-6 tells us

5 Trust in the Lord with all your heart and lean not on your own understanding; 6 in all your ways submit to him, and he will make your paths straight.

When we rely on our own strength and wisdom instead of God's, we end up taking long, winding paths that lead us to self-destruction and heartbreak. Only when we rely on God and trust Him and His direction does he make our paths straight and show us where we should go. Even though I wasn't fully relying on God at the time, and even though there was chaos all around me, I knew He would take care of me and my baby. Jose and I were still stubbornly trying to write our own story and pave our own way, which led to messy paths, but trust me, *God can redeem all stories and all journeys.*

Where in your own life have you sought approval or comfort on your own terms? Where have you decided what your future would hold and paid a high price to make it so? Are you trapped in a mess of your own making? Take heart. There is *no* mess my God cannot turn into a masterpiece! How He does it is a mystery, but you can trust His process.

4

SEEKING STABILITY

That summer living with Jose was so full! We lived life in fast-forward, trying to fit in everything we could before the baby came. The kids would spend weekends with us, the girls especially. They enjoyed the idea of a new baby and would spend time practicing with dolls, touching my stomach, feeling the baby kick, and even looking "into" my belly button to "see" the baby. The boys were a different story. Being older, they understood more of the rift that was happening in their family. They saw their mom sad all the time and had no interest in being around pregnant me and their father. It was easier with the girls since they were little and didn't understand the messiness of the situation. Their ignorance helped us ignore reality too. I had a lot of fun playing house with Jose. He is a really good dad, and even those days it was obvious how much he genuinely enjoyed spending time with his kids. His favorite days were when it was the two of us with all his kids and that gave me hope. It made it easy to think eventually, our twisted, delusional fantasy for the future could actually work out.

In the fall of 2006, it was time for my daughter to be born. I wasn't feeling a lot of contractions or pain, but everything was uncomfortable. Sitting, standing, lying down, it all felt like pressure. On my birthday, I was woken up around five in the morning with contractions. After two hours, I drove myself to the hospital in the manual transmission truck. If you're a parent, you may already expect what I'm going to say next. As soon as I started checking in, the contractions slowed down. By ten o'clock that morning, they had stopped, and the nurses sent me home. I'd not progressed dilation, I was not going to give birth that day. I spent the day feeling like I'd failed again. I began to be afraid this was a sign of what type of mother I would be, incapable of doing what was needed. I called my mom, and she, of course, made the drive down to be with me. She explained again that the contractions I was feeling were commonly known as Braxton Hicks, sort of practice contractions, and how no two pregnancies are the same. Mom reminded me that what I'd read and researched might feel different than it was described. She also encouraged me that usually, the symptoms I was experiencing were all signs that the baby would arrive any day! For the next two weeks, she walked with me and walked and walked and walked with me.

My actual due date came and to the doctor's we went. After all the miles of walking to help things along, I was still not anywhere close to starting labor. We decided to induce after the weekend on Tuesday morning. If I could go back in time, I'd tell myself to wait it out, but then I was so impatient. After the induction appointment was set, my father joined us in Georgia so he could be there to meet his new granddaughter. Tuesday came, and my parents, Jose, and I went to the hospital and got things rolling. I was so excited to meet my baby finally. I wouldn't go home empty-handed this time. I would get it right. Things were ok for a long while as I waited and waited for the medication to do its thing. I was frustrated but not in any pain. Things were mostly going well until they suddenly weren't. A nurse came in at one point after my epidural to help me change positions so they could find the baby's heartbeat again, which thankfully they did, scaring me very much in the process. Finally, some hours later, it was time to push.

FINALLY A MOM

My daughter came out perfectly into the world early on a Wednesday morning. She was beautiful and all mine. I saw her for just a minute or two before they whisked her away. I was so proud and so exhausted and I kept bleeding. Birth is a messy process, and supposedly, a woman's body is supposed to know what to do. After all the medication to induce labor, my body no longer knew what step we were on. The nurses kept me together until the doctor, who was across town at another delivery, arrived just in time to stop the bleeding and get me stabilized. I think I slept for an entire day while all my blood levels came back to normal. When I finally had strength enough back, they brought me my daughter. I could have stared at her forever. It was all worth it. I fell completely in love with her and I never wanted to be apart from her. She was just everything to me. We had made it through a long, hard nine months together and an eventful birth process, but we were leaving the hospital together and healthy. My parents stayed with us for a few more days, but within a week, things had to get back to routine.

As 2006 came to a close, I was barely twenty-one years old and a new mom, not just of one baby but, depending on the weekend, three to five children. I worked hard to play the part of a good partner and not make any more trouble for Jose than I already had just by existing. He and his wife legally separated, but the arguments didn't stop. Trying to spend time together usually got interrupted by an emergency, and our weekends with the kids typically had an explosive, toxic end. As much as they loved their dad and sister, Jose's children didn't always want to be around me. The oldest was ten years old, and the youngest was nearly two years old. They didn't understand how their family was changing or why this was happening to them. We still managed to make a lot of good memories. The boys played baseball and football and there was always something to do. Oftentimes, with seemingly no warning, Jose would get a phone call, and his wife would announce she was coming to take the kids back early. This always seemed to happen on our best weekends with them, even once when my parents were visiting. Jose and his wife would fight and argue for long bouts, usually in another room or outside, away from me. It began to feel like a pattern Jose's wife was doing purposefully just to be spiteful.

I couldn't understand why she wouldn't just admit defeat. It seemed so simple to me. She hadn't been happy in the marriage either. Why couldn't she just try to move on herself instead of making everyone as miserable as she was? Jose and the kids might not be having fun with her around but at least they weren't having fun with me either. I felt like I was the source of nothing but problems, but I was not allowed to be part of the solution or even the conversation. Jose was taking hits from all sides: his sons, his wife, and even his extended family members. Jose intended to shield me from the attacks and bear it all himself. He felt like his pushing for us to be together had put me in an awful position so he could at least protect me from the direct blows. Despite his best efforts, I still felt the ire from everyone around us and it was infuriating to feel kept on the sidelines like a child. I made so many mistakes. I was petty and even mean. I didn't like who I was and the reasons why I was staying with Jose got a little blurred.

Facing life and the trials of life on our own will always leave us burnt out, short-changed, and broken. We cannot schedule, organize, self-help, or otherwise force our way into stability in life. Only through the inner peace that Holy Spirit brings, the shalom that the Bible describes, can we experience stability through the chaos of life. Shalom means nothing missing and nothing broken. It is found only in the presence of Jesus. I was NOT ready to invite God into my mess. For all I knew, He wanted nothing to do with me anymore. 1 Peter 5:10 promises us:

10 (And) the God of all grace, who called you to his eternal glory in Christ, after you have suffered a little while, will himself restore you and make you strong, firm and steadfast.

I was too busy ignoring God and anything to do with Jesus or Holy Spirit to invite His presence and peace into the chaos around me. I felt weak, broken, confused, and lonely, and needed something to change. Maybe you can understand feeling desperation mingled with anger and stubbornness. Regardless of how hopeless you may feel, I believe as you read these pages that the light of hope has been ignited and will continue to grow.

5

SEEKING HELP

About a year after our daughter was born, Jose and I nearly broke up. I still believed I was the cause of all the pain and drama we were living through. Jose's kids were hurting. Jose's wife was hurting. Jose's family was constantly having me thrown in their face and my very presence was offensive to them. Jose was hurting and couldn't talk to me about it because he didn't want me to feel worse. His wife and the kids had moved out of state to be with her family and Jose had never been apart from his kids that far or for that long. He made trips to see them every weekend and sometimes I was allowed to go, but it was extremely tense. These were some of the darkest, worst months of our entire relationship. I was so alone, so afraid of setting off the people around me, so on guard all the time, and never a true version of myself. I lived to make the people in the room around me happy. That felt like the best thing I could do, considering they were being forced to tolerate my presence. I was the stray dog that just kept hanging around but nobody wanted.

My daughter was my only bright spot and I was so cautious with her. I was privileged to watch her develop and grow despite all my shortcomings. She was loved by her extended family and by her siblings, and while I was her mother, I was also wicked. I stayed so she could be a part of a big, strong family with values I agreed with. It wasn't fun how they treated me, but what else could I expect? I was the mistress. I busted up a family. I was not their blood. Jose was focused on his kids; it didn't feel right to ask for anything for myself. I was utterly alone.

During the months right around my daughter's first birthday, I happened to hit it off with a guy at work who didn't have any attachments, no baggage I cared to know about, and he thought I was pretty. It was fun to flirt, to laugh, to feel seen and a bit like the old me who knew what fun was. I found myself looking for control again, trying to find my bearings in a life that had gotten away from me again. Just like all the times before, I dove into moral failure, into a sexual encounter, because at least that outcome was predictable. I could control that. On a work trip, after too much to drink, I cheated on Jose. Worse than that, when I got home from the work trip, I tried to maintain contact with this guy and hide it.

When I left work one day to pick up my daughter from day-care like usual, she wasn't there. I was told that her dad had already picked her up. When I arrived home, my belongings had been thrown into two large garbage bags outside our apartment. Jose and I proceeded to have several hard, somewhat scary conversations. Jose would not be separated from another child and told me I could leave if I wanted but it would be without my daughter. That was not an option for me. I would rather stay with her no matter what, and I didn't want to leave Jose. I loved him, I'd just felt so far from him, so alone. I was so guilty, ashamed, and afraid, but I agreed with Jose that my loneliness was not an excuse to seek comfort elsewhere. How could I have made things so much worse? I even tried to make things fair and square between Jose and me by finding a random girl on a dating site for Jose to pursue. He did have a date with her but told me that he couldn't go through with anything physical with her, though she had been willing. How noble was he? And how lucky could I be?

I signed back up for the package deal of Jose and all his kids and all the mess because, after all, it was the mess we had created together. We were going to see it through, not run away. How cowardly of me to run away! What had I been thinking? I reminded myself what a treasure it was to be with a man who loved his kids and wanted them. He was in pain because he was a good father who was being kept from his kids because of me. I couldn't take away the one child he could see every day. I convinced myself that I was unable to make good decisions and that it would be better to let someone else call the shots. We decided that instead of throwing me out, I'd be allowed to stay so that all the naysayers wouldn't be proven right.

DESPERATE TO BE ANYONE ELSE

Staying through the emotional neglect and verbal abuse was the only way I could stay with my daughter because I refused to leave her or take her away from her dad. Now I really couldn't make any mistakes, but I also shouldn't be too happy. How could I live with myself? Every day, I had to prove I was sorry. Anything could be a reason showing I didn't want to be there. If I said I'd get the laundry or dishes done and forgot to get to them, it'd be because I was planning to leave or because I had no respect for Jose. If dinner wasn't made or the kids were not attended to, it was because I wanted out. I was never thanked for anything I did; it was owed to Jose for what I'd done. Jose still loved me, and his presence was proof enough of that. I still loved Jose and I was desperately trying to survive loving him and being a good girlfriend and partner through a mountain of self-loathing.

Later, in the year 2007, I ended up in a behavioral therapist's office and was diagnosed with major depression and prescribed daily medication. I described to the doctor that I felt like I made everything worse for everyone around me. I didn't want to end my life but I resented where I'd ended up and wanted to disappear. Out of my self-resentment and self-hatred, I lashed out at others and sabotaged myself. Even after cheating on him, I had never been "too much" for Jose, like I'd been for other people, but I renewed every effort and certainly tried to be. If he sent me away or left me, then I could continue to be the victim —- I would have my out. I could tell people that it was just too hard. But he didn't send me away. He wasn't going to let me tuck tail and leave with our daughter. We didn't handle it in a Christlike manner but Jose fought for me and us when I'd quit.

DIGGING OUR HEELS IN

I couldn't see past how awful I was, taking on the blame for everything bad that had happened and masking my true feelings to keep moving forward. Jose and I agreed that we weren't going to let what everybody expected to happen to us come true. We held the pen to our epic story and we'd continue to write our own narrative. I stayed through a lot of emotional turmoil and messiness because I felt I deserved it. The depression medication helped keep me from reacting rashly —- it kept me level-headed and helped me not feel my pain —- but it did nothing to address or heal the identity-crushing wounds I was experiencing and excusing. I was reminded of the things that had been said about me by the leaders at church and in my discipleship program, and now, after all I'd done, didn't they have to be right? I thought about what Jose's family thought about me and what they had said to him to warn him about me. Hadn't I proved what they said was true? I might as well stop fighting it and stop trying to be good. I tried to embrace the horrible person I must really be. I tried to present the image that I was who I was, take it or leave it, but the image I was trying to present was not a person I liked, and not who I am, but I tried to make it true for a long, long, exhausting time.

Again, if I had reached out to God at this time, I would have experienced Psalm 34:18, which promises that:

18 The Lord is close to the brokenhearted;
he rescues those whose spirits are crushed.

There are many solutions the world offers us in our times of need: distractions, products, strategies, life hacks, therapists, gurus, and coaches. None of these "solutions" are inherently bad, but the world's solutions are only treating the symptoms and not the root. When we are desperate for help, only turning to Jesus will give us the help and hope we need to keep moving forward. I was not yet ready to turn to Jesus for help. I had been so hurt by the church and so stubborn in my ways that I thought I could do this whole life thing on my own. But I kept facing trials that were slowly breaking down my self-dependency.

6
SEEKING SHELTER

So far, that was just our first year together. The next nine years were just as emotionally messy, but we tried to focus on the good parts. We made a life together with the kids. Jose and his wife divorced in 2011, five years after our daughter was born. After the divorce was finalized, some things in how we governed the home changed, but I was still just the girlfriend. I couldn't help Jose with the kids like he wanted me to because I had no authority to talk to doctors or teachers. I couldn't have a conversation with Jose's ex-wife about handling things with the kids because one or both of us would be petty and cause trouble. Things had changed forever between Jose and me after my affair —- he never looked at me the same and his priority was focused explicitly on his kids. The kids and I had our good days and lots of bad days. My stepsons, now fifteen and ten, were more or less easy. I didn't attempt to parent them really, just hang out and get to know them.

I learned to play video games, but not well, and fell in love with the Harry Potter series. My stepdaughters were another story. They were eight and six by this time and didn't remember life without me in it. They knew Mom and Dad fought a lot when they were together, but particularly, the girls, understandably, wanted their parents to be around at the same time. It was very confusing for them. On more than one occasion, when told "no," they would announce defiantly that I was not their mother and that they didn't have to listen to me. Who knows if this was a result of their mom telling them this, the hands-off approach I was supposed to take with them, or just normal hard-headed kid behavior. Regardless of where it came from, as an insecure twenty-two-year-old, I did not handle it well. I took it personally and allowed the girls to become more voices confirming my worthlessness. I was stuck between hanging on for the good moments because they were so good and enduring the rough ones. I had to be grateful, after all, since I was a Jezebel, an adulterer, a home wrecker. This was the best I could hope for and didn't deserve any better. I'd better just shut up and enjoy what moments I could.

TROUBLE UPON TROUBLE

One day I got a phone call from Jose's mom letting me know that he and his brother had been in a terrible car accident. They were both okay, all things considered, but Jose left the hospital with a hip joint out of the socket and nerve damage in his knee, as well as a contusion on the entire right side of his head that affected his memory. While we were in the hospital, Jose's memory seemed to only last for a minute or two. He knew who I was but his timeline was confused. The kids' ages were all jumbled out of order. Jose would ask a series of questions and just when we got him calmed down, he would forget and cycle back through the same questions.

For a long time after the accident, memories would come flooding back as if they were brand new and at random moments. I quietly hoped he would never remember that I'd cheated on him or the messiness that followed. His memory, even in the short term, would come and go. I remember preparing for a softball tournament and leaving to buy groceries. When I returned with the bags, Jose had forgotten why I'd left and was upset that I had been gone so long and had bought stuff. Despite how she felt about me, one of his sisters spoke up and helped me out then and reminded him that he had sent me to buy the snacks for the tournament. Everything was still wonky and chaotic. It was hard to feel any stability from one day to the next. Our lives were like a boat on a stormy sea, tossed around by the wind and waves.

The year following Jose's car accident, we had another catastrophe. Our home had been built in the 1970s and I think we still had the original gas stove. The knobs for the eyes were in the front and it was very easy to bump them, turn the gas on and even hear the clicking of the stove trying to ignite. I happened to make a baked fish one evening —- just lemon pepper on a frozen filet, nothing fancy. When we left for the various sports practices happening that night, I left a couple of pieces of leftover fish on the stove and thought nothing of it. Either I bumped the stove knobs on the way out of the house, or our dog, typically the best-behaved dog in the world, must have turned the stove on, reaching up to get at the fish. The firemen were able to tell us that the fire started at the stove, the pot of cooking oil on the back eye eventually going off like a bomb. Thankfully, no one was home, and our dog was smart enough to seek shelter under a bed downstairs but the whole house burned up. A neighbor called the firemen and they busted in to search since the neighbors knew children lived at the home. They found and resuscitated our dog, who lived through the experience nearly unscathed. We saved a few bags of clothes and my photo albums. Sometimes I still find myself looking for something and remembering we lost it in the fire. Our family took us in temporarily and the community pulled together to support and help us. One family we knew through our daughter's T-ball teams even let us live in their house that they had listed on the market but hadn't gotten much interest.

This huge house was an amazing gift, but it was forty-five minutes away from where we had lived in the house that had burned down. Jose, keeping a promise to his son, left the house at 5:30 am to take the kids to the same school rather than transfer them in the middle of the school year, and then he went to work. Then they completed their after-school activities and came home around 11 pm. Rinse and repeat Monday to Friday. The goal and the promise were not to punish the kids by disrupting their routines. It didn't feel fair for them to have to face loss again after already having gone through so much. The cost of making sure the kids were catered to was that I was left alone, with our dog, in an enormous house all day. I loved that dog so much, and we became the best of friends during those long days of only each other to be with, but distance grew again between Jose and me. I made trips out of state with our daughter back to my hometown every weekend. For nearly a year, while they rebuilt our burned-down house, Jose and I barely saw each other.

This was the second dark period together, again because we were emotionally distanced from each other and didn't make time to communicate. This time around I was the one who was traveling out of state every weekend. My time with my family was relaxing and I enjoyed the simplicity of just having my daughter to care for. I drank too much alcohol and even hid smoking cigarettes from Jose. There was one particular drive leaving my hometown to return to Jose in Georgia, where I cried for what felt like the entire six-hour trip. I felt trapped and confused, definitely unhappy but lost on what to do next. I somehow found the courage to ask Jose the question that was ever present in my mind: Why hadn't he proposed, even though his divorce had been finalized? He told me he still wasn't ready to be married again. That he wasn't sure he'd ever be. I remember he said, "I could get you a ring to buy some more time because you'd be happy with the sparkles, but I want to do things right by you this time." I was devastated. It sounded like the old spin doctor Jose telling me whatever it took to end the conversation like he had done before I moved back to Georgia to give birth to our daughter. Where did that leave me? What had I done? I was trapped but I was not going to live this way. I began to fantasize about how to leave and take my daughter with me.

A NEW ESCAPE

I hoped my relationship with Jose would improve when we moved back into our rebuilt house, and when moving day came, I was so excited to be back home and together again. I assumed that now that the commute was much shorter, we'd feel like a family again, or at least whatever version of family we had been pretending to be. Strangely enough, nothing seemed to change. Jose was still gone a lot, prioritizing the kids' activities and the two of us just playing taxi. I remember telling him one day in August 2012, while I cried into the pot of spaghetti I was poorly cooking, that I couldn't be his girlfriend anymore. I couldn't be a roommate to help with the kids and keep his bed warm. We had spent six years together following the storyline we were writing for ourselves, working awkwardly toward the goal Jose had kept in sight all along: custody of all his kids and me at his side. And we had it! We should have been happy having reached what we had worked so long for. I found I could fake it in most situations, especially around other people, but the journey to having everything we wanted had left us both so changed in each other's eyes. Now more than ever, we seemed to be staying together only to prevent the naysayers from being right about us and our future. Haven't you done that too? Haven't you held onto something you knew was not good for you just to spite someone else? How often do we allow something to stay in our lives because of pride? It happens sometimes when you're playing poker. A hand comes along that looks like it has potential, so you bet many chips. As the hand continues, it gets to a point when you have already bet so much that even if you want to fold, it feels too late to. They call it being pot-committed. We know we aren't going to win the hand, but we might as well stay in it in case all we've put into it pays off. This is where I found myself. This hand no longer looked as good as when it first started, and I wanted to fold, but I wasn't sure how to make the call. I told Jose that night in August, after making arguably the worst pot of spaghetti in the history of the meal, that I wanted to take my daughter and leave him, but I couldn't bear leaving the kids. In the process of gaining custody of the kids, the girls especially had been confused and often felt abandoned by their mother. She had made an extremely difficult sacrifice for what she believed was the best for her kids' stability, a sacrifice I couldn't imagine making.

The nature of the life we had created seemed to have no winners. It was a mess for everyone: Jose, his ex-wife, and definitely for their kids. So, I lay upstairs with Jose in our bed that night in August, calmly explaining what I'd spent months wrestling with. I did not want to be with him but I couldn't make sense of leaving his kids. I didn't want to take my daughter away from her siblings or her extended family. Regardless of how they felt about me, they loved her and were good to her. I was tortured, miserable, and tired of being miserable. There wasn't anyone else, no one in my hometown that I wanted to be with — I just didn't want to be with Jose anymore. I was done. I explained this without tears or hysterics. I wasn't angry. I was just done and felt stuck. Jose responded by letting me know he had recently decided he was ready to propose, just that he wanted to plan it out and make it special. I laughed at him and told him he was too late. I'd wanted to hear that for so long, but I didn't care anymore. Jose asked if he could try to fix it, which certainly helped my moral dilemma about the kids. So, I agreed that he could try.

All the transitions in life, all the chaos around me, made me feel isolated and alone. It's natural to seek shelter during storms to keep ourselves safe and grounded. During trials in life, the only safe shelter we can seek is in God's presence, but I still wasn't ready to reach out to Him. I was still angry and stiff-necked to do things my way. Jesus is waiting to be our safeguard and He can help us withstand all that life and the enemy throw at us. James 1:2-4 tells us:

2 Consider it pure joy, my brothers and sisters, whenever you face trials of many kinds, 3 because you know that the testing of your faith produces perseverance. 4 Let perseverance finish its work so that you may be mature and complete, not lacking anything.

And in Matthew 7:24-27 Jesus says:

24 Everyone then who hears these words of mine and does them will be like a wise man who built his house on the rock. 25 And the rain fell, and the floods came, and the winds blew and beat on that house, but it did not fall, because it had been founded on the rock. 26 And everyone who hears these words of mine and does not do them will be like a foolish man who built his house on the sand. 27 And the rain fell, and the floods came, and the winds blew and beat against that house, and it fell, and great was the fall of it.

As long as you carry on thinking you know best, thinking you are the author of your story, your life is pretty much guaranteed to be a mess. Your best will be based on your knowledge, your experiences, and your hopes. Such things are vastly limited when compared to the omniscience of your Creator, God. I admit now that I was such a fool, barely surviving the storms of life and experiencing one great fall after another. I had very little hope for the future but soldiered on. The way I saw it, if things between Jose and me happened to get any worse, then I'd have my excuse to leave. If things miraculously got better, then I might just end up with a life like I wanted all along. Beyond any reason that makes sense, I agreed to let Jose try to fix our relationship and I stayed a little longer.

7

SEEKING SECURITY

Amazingly, after a few awkward days, we were so much better. I felt valued, seen, and loved again. There were small adjustments Jose made to prioritize me and what I needed. I wasn't second to the kids and didn't feel like a roommate or nanny anymore. It seemed unlikely and miraculous after things had been so bad for so long, but everything had changed. I finally had hope again. Things weren't perfect, but I wasn't going anywhere.

Jose and I have since learned about communication in relationships, and what I know now is a good explanation for how, in the world, things could change so drastically and so quickly. There are several ways people communicate, but two very basic types of communication are topically and relationally. Most arguments or disagreements happen when one person is speaking topically, and the other receives a relational message from it. For example, in the wintertime, like most women, I shave my legs less often. I'm typically bundled up in long pants and multiple pairs of socks. It's very practical that since my legs are not visible to the general public, I save time in the shower and skip shaving as often. Although people outside the house don't see my bare legs, Jose still does. So, topically and logically, it's understandable why I wouldn't shave as often in the winter, but relationally, Jose received the message that I cared more about presenting my best self to people outside the house than to him.

When I was all smiles and extroverted in public but then hardly said a word at home, it sent Jose the same message. Topically, I feel like I should be safe at home just to exist; whereas in certain public settings, I'm required to be engaging for the sake of others. Relationally, Jose felt like I was giving my best to strangers and my leftovers to him. While the defensive thought was to be confused and frustrated that Jose would be upset over what I felt was so trivial, that only led to us being at odds with each other. We had to learn to hear each other and seek to understand. These kinds of topical and relational communication discrepancies happened often with Jose and I both taking turns on which side of the argument we were on.

There are a million examples from our lives and other couples we have spoken with that I could share. If you're in a close relationship with anyone, not just as a couple, then I'm sure you can think of examples from your own life. It's easy and common to feel like you and the other person are speaking different languages. If all we wanted was to be right in an argument, then that's all we won. When we began to seek understanding of the other person, we realized our relationship was stronger for it, and we both won! Jose and I developed what we call a "home team" —- an effort to put our relationship and each other first. We, as a unified front, mattered more than the individual. We put effort into celebrating, supporting, and understanding each other. Things weren't immediately perfect but we were working together on us. It wasn't just about the kids or taxiing them around to their activities. I felt seen and heard, valued as part of the family and not just a cog in the wheel. Our lives were made richer because we worked toward our future together instead of just surviving the present.

Then, out of nowhere, something jogged Jose's memory, and he not only remembered my affair but also the worst parts of the beginnings of our relationship. When he let me know he had remembered, I was terrified. Were things going to go back to how they had been? Was I going to have to jump ship after all? But a miracle was happening. Jose now saw that time through fresh eyes and with a new perspective. He could understand what I must have felt even without my trying to explain it to him. He truly forgave me and was open to talking through what had happened to us.

Please understand what I'm saying here. My response to the painful results of our choices, choosing to look outside the relationship for relief from what was happening in the relationship, was a hundred percent wrong. The incredible thing to be learned here was that the time we had spent investing in the idea of a "home team" was not wasted. Jose actually apologized to me for things he had done and said and promised to remain different, to love me better. I was speechless.

We were still living according to our own rules, without consulting or including Jesus, but it seemed for the first time in years that my relationship with Jose could actually work out. We were a united front, valuing one another and doing the daily work to keep the communication open. We were still living by our own rules, never consulting or including Jesus, but for the first time in years, it felt like my relationship with José might actually work out. We had become a united front—valuing each other, communicating openly, and doing the daily work to keep our household in order.

It seemed as though we had cracked the code, figured out how to succeed without God. And we were so proud of it.

We mocked the church and its people, convinced we were better—wiser, more grounded, more in tune with reality. We had built what we thought was a *beautiful* life, one that followed the basic structure of godly principles but without acknowledging the God who had established them. We took all the credit for ourselves. And we were loud about it. We bragged to anyone who would listen, convinced that our way was superior. Success, as we defined it, was about self-reliance—carrying everything on your own because, after all, who else would? No one was coming to save you. No one else cared as much as you did.

Unfortunately, the circumstances around us only seemed to confirm this belief.

One day, José's oldest son told us that one of his friends—who had been crashing on our couch for a couple of days—had been kicked out of his house. He was just fifteen. He was the most polite, sweet-natured, soft-spoken kid. What could he have possibly done to warrant being thrown out like that?

We decided to meet with his mother, thinking we could help reconcile the family. After all, we were *so* wise, weren't we? We had all of our kids at home, so surely, we knew how to manage difficult family dynamics.

To this day, I am still baffled by that meeting. For all my flaws and failures at the time, I *could not* understand a mother abandoning her child. I couldn't even fathom abandoning José's kids, let alone my own. But everyone is wired differently, and Jesus died to save all kinds. Even still, this woman... she was something else.

She agreed—without hesitation—for her son to live with us. With strangers. The plan was to give them six weeks apart, time to cool down. She described him as rebellious, defiant, unwilling to listen. We took him in, promising ourselves that this was temporary, that we'd help mend their relationship. Six weeks later, we met again. Sitting across from her son, she looked him in the eyes and, with chilling indifference, said she didn't want him back. I was furious. But I swallowed my rage, took the young man by the hand, and brought him home. He was ours now.

From that point forward, we communicated with his mother only through email, arranging to gather the rest of his things—birth certificate, health insurance, social security information. In the process, we met with DFACS, only to learn that there was already a file on him. There had been previous reports of abuse. Then came another discovery. When we finally received his birth certificate, we realized he was a year older than he had been told. That year, he got two birthday cakes—one for each year he had lived without knowing who he truly was. As for the so-called rebellion his mother had accused him of? It turned out he had simply refused to steal. His mother and her boyfriend had sent him out to rob his friends, and when he got caught—or when he refused to do it—he was beaten, sometimes to the point of unconsciousness. There was no question. He would stay with us.

We refused to let him fend for himself, especially when it was clear that DFACS had done little to protect him. The church he had once been part of had also failed him. When I asked if anyone at church had noticed the bruises, if anyone had ever tried to help, he simply shook his head.

"They saw," he told me. "But they never asked."

They had accepted whatever cover story they had been given. And for me, this was just more ammunition against the church. I remember the day he asked if he could go back. I didn't just say no—I berated him for even considering it.

"Why?" I demanded. "Why would you open yourself up to more pain? They didn't do anything for you when you needed them. You *don't* need church. You're better off without fake people in your life."

I was so blinded by my own pain that I couldn't see what I was doing to those around me. On the surface, we had done a good thing. We had taken in a child, given him safety, and provided for his needs. But good deeds without the right heart are like building on sand. It may hold for a while, but eventually, the foundation gives way. And that's exactly where we were headed—toward a collapse we didn't see coming.

Sometime later, Jose planned a beautiful proposal on Christmas day, 2012, in the Sacred Plaza on top of Machu Picchu in Peru while we were traveling there with his entire family. I was over the moon, and we began planning the wedding of our dreams, complete with a taco bar and a nacho cheese fountain!

Our wedding day went mostly as planned, and we had an incredible time celebrating the next chapter of our epic love story. We had made it through hell and back. There had been so much in our lives that had tried to tear us apart, but we persevered and stayed together against all odds. I was so genuinely happy to be Jose's wife and to carry his name. I still am! So much was going well for us, but just under the surface, we were still so broken and angry. Our strength and sense of wholeness came entirely from each other, despite knowing the dangers of that kind of co-dependence. The pen writing our story was still in our hands as we fumbled through, doing our best with short-sighted vision and asking no one for help. We could at least admit that God had provided for us and our family even though we had not been actively seeking Him. Even though we had been trying to write our own story, we slowly realized God's hand in all of this. He had determined that our running season was over, and it was time to return home. Jeremiah 29:11 tells us:

29 For I know the plans I have for you, declares the Lord, plans for welfare and not for evil, to give you a future and a hope.

Sometimes it's hard to trust that God has our best interests at heart. We need the security of knowing what's next. But God has proven Himself faithful time and time again throughout Scripture and in the lives of countless believers. We can trust that He has a plan for our lives that is hopeful.

Part Two

GOD'S REWRITE

8

FINDING PEACE

"Put it in the book!" Jose would often tease me as we "wrote" our own rules for what our lives would be like together. From early in our relationship, we had determined that we were going to take on the world together. We didn't need anybody but each other and thought we were happy. When I think back on those years, I can smile at the good stuff but shake my head at the masks we wore and the bravado we blustered to cover our hurt and shame. We thought our epic love story was going to be us against the world, depending only on ourselves. We spent ten long years lost and angry, mad at God and mad at the church, but one day everything changed. On Easter Sunday, 2015, we uneasily made our way to Discover Life Church. We had decided to go to thank God because, despite our anger, we recognized that He had continued to protect us. Somehow our bills got paid even when the math for the month didn't add up. All our children were growing up safe, fed, and had their needs met.

So, we went to church, fully anticipating hating every moment and never going back. After all, we said, even the heathens go to church on Easter. So when we don't show up again, no one will notice! The pastor was beginning a series called "This is Jesus" and gently reintroduced us to who Jesus is and how much He loves us. He has been waiting, like the prodigal son's father, to welcome us back home to Him. Instead of the Sunday we were expecting, we were met by nothing but open arms, old friends, and warm smiles. It was incredibly surprising and humbling and terrifying. When we walked up, and I recognized the greeter at the door, I nearly ran away. Remember, I'd been told that I was a problem and that I was not welcome in the church because of the damage I'd done and inevitably would do again.

Nevertheless, this couple met us at the door and pulled us in. They were so happy to see us and it seemed genuine. Not one person gave me the dirty looks I was anticipating. The following week, Jose and I tried to think of a reason not to go back, but we honestly couldn't. Something had awoken in our spirits, and despite being extremely uncomfortable, we both admitted we missed God's presence more than we realized. Still, the road ahead was not an easy one for us. I couldn't worship. Partly because it had been a decade, and I didn't know the lyrics to the worship songs, but mostly because of the unworthiness I felt. I couldn't say those words on the screen without feeling condemned and ashamed. I was still too much of a hypocrite to sing those words. I didn't mean them yet. So I stood stiff and frozen, not singing, just crying. The pastor would take the stage and begin to speak and I would cry more. For at least the first month, all I could do in the service was cry. Jose would accidentally bump me or touch my hand and I would pull away. On one occasion, he leaned over to remind me that we were married now and that I was safe, but I couldn't shake the feeling that stones of judgment were in the hands of the people around me.

PERSPECTIVE SHIFTING

It's truly amazing looking back on the years of my life and seeing how God was with us all along, protecting us from going too far off the deep end. We always had food on the table and the bills always seemed to get paid. Our kids were protected and healthy. Things on the outside looked pretty good. God's mercy was extended to us so far beyond what we could fathom. My spirit trembling inside me must have known the precarious situation I was putting myself in to enter the presence of The Holy God. When people in the Bible, both Old and New Testaments, treated the sacred presence of God with familiarity, as if it were common, as if their sin were an exception to the rule, they were struck dead! I believe the prayers of my mother and the compassion that greeted us at Discover Life Church saved our lives. Like in Exodus 32, when Moses pleaded for God not to wipe out Israel after they made and worshiped the golden calf, Jose and I were shown incredible mercy because others had been praying on our behalf. Exodus 32:9-14 says:

9 "I have seen these people," the Lord said to Moses, "and they are a stiff-necked people. 10 Now leave me alone so that my anger may burn against them and that I may destroy them. Then I will make you into a great nation." 11 But Moses sought the favor of the Lord his God. "Lord ," he said, "why should your anger burn against your people, whom you brought out of Egypt with great power and a mighty hand? 12 Why should the Egyptians say, 'It was with evil intent that he brought them out, to kill them in the mountains and to wipe them off the face of the earth'? Turn from your fierce anger; relent and do not bring disaster on your people. 13 Remember your servants Abraham, Isaac and Israel, to whom you swore by your own self: 'I will make your descendants as numerous as the stars in the sky and I will give your descendants all this land I promised them, and it will be their inheritance forever.'" 14 Then the Lord relented and did not bring on his people the disaster he had threatened.

That first sermon series was entitled "This is Jesus" and was designed to reintroduce the congregation to who God is, how much He loves us, and His design for us without the mess of human intervention complicating things. What a perfect message to woo my wounded and deceived heart back into the Kingdom! I remember we'd come in late, find our seats in the sanctuary, I'd weep for the hour, and then we'd go home as quickly as possible. I stood stiff during worship because I felt so unworthy of worship. How could I raise my voice to sing to Jesus? How could I lift my hands or express worship with my body, which for the last ten years had been used to express such a different message? To see me worship now in that kind of posture may be hard to believe. I most definitely wanted to be at church, but I just felt so dirty, so unworthy, and so hypocritical. It took a long time for me to trust the church people, especially the women, but it did happen. God gently restored and healed our hearts and brought us back into His family.

Eventually, we asked to meet with the lead pastors at their home. We wanted to tell them our story and tell them who we'd been. If it was not okay for us to be there, I wanted to find out sooner than later before we got any more attached. We asked for the "Twelve Steps to Restoration" so that we could be in right standing with Jesus. We were prepared to hear that we could not be together because our marriage, as a second marriage and because of the affair, could never be in right standing with Jesus. I was not sure what we would decide if that was the case. Jose and I both hoped they wouldn't say that, but we agreed to hear them out. God was already pulling on our hearts, and being in His presence was taking more and more priority. Jose and I knew that we wanted to have a real, authentic, complete relationship with Jesus. We wanted to do it for real this time, and we talked about our confusion about what to do if God asked us to give each other up. Surely He wouldn't bust up another family, we told ourselves. Surely He wouldn't force Jose and Robin to reconcile their marriage. We had no answers, but with trepidation, we were asking questions.

Our pastors told us something revolutionary — Jesus just wanted us. He wanted a yes in our hearts for His will and His purposes. We were advised to keep a yes in our hearts for Him. Practically, that looked like a simple posture change to lift our palms. Symbolically, even with arms at our sides, the change from clenched fists to open palms helped us engage openly with Holy Spirit. It was simple, and it was a beginning — a small gesture, to be sure, but the Bible tells us not to despise small beginnings. The only thing we had to do was say 'YES!' Yes to the love of Jesus Christ. Yes, to His sacrifice for us. From there, we took things day by day, continuing to be open to where God was leading us with a yes in our hearts.

To anyone wrestling with letting go of something for the sake of taking hold of Christ, my advice is just to pursue Him anyway. Come to Him as you are, and share your heart authentically with Him by asking the hard questions and admitting what He already knows you're struggling with. Then let Him answer your questions. Listen for His voice and let Him lead you in what His will is for you. The simple fact is that Christ loves us and that we do not have to do anything to earn it. In our case, God did not ask Jose and me to give each other up. His plan of restoration kept us together in marriage. That doesn't mean His plan was easy or that our beginnings had been signed off on. Our sin was not okay. We were covered in God's mercy and committed to the hard work of becoming who He created us to be despite all the detours and roadblocks we had put in our own way. God was faithful to pick up the pen and rewrite our story.

This meeting was the first time we had heard the concept of "being and doing" from a pastor. We had never before considered that it was important first to know our identity, who Jesus says we are, and that out of that identity, we overflow into doing good through the empowerment of Holy Spirit. They explained that Jesus' love for us was truly unconditional and that in His death on the cross, He had paid the penalty for all our sins. The wrath of God was satisfied and our debt had been covered. There was nothing we could do or should do to earn His forgiveness or a place in the church. This was just the beginning for us.

TAKING STEPS FORWARD

One day I called my pastor for help. I was angry. Every time I drove by our former church, which during that season was twice a day, I felt deep hatred welling up in me. I had been robbed of myself. I was lied to and hurt for what reason? As I was getting close to God again I was reminded of who I'd been, moments when I had experienced Jesus, but were they even real? What could I trust? What was the truth? And how dare these people at my former church twist things up so badly for a teenager who was excited and hungry and seeking God! Who did they think they were? Who did I think I was? After all, I'd made my own terrible choices. No one had forced those choices on me.

As you can see, there was a pretty big pretzel in my head. I had no clarity except that it was painfully clear I was angry. My pastor agreed to meet with me and asked my permission to invite another counselor, to which I agreed. I was headed once again to meet with two female leaders in the church, neither of whom I had a deep relationship with, and I was really scared of what they'd say.

Despite my fear, I was more hungry for change. I knew I was damaged. I knew I was hurting. I had no idea how much healing and transformation I needed and this was just the beginning. I still carry the truths revealed that day that my pastor wrote down for me in my Bible like a monument of what God began for me that day. I experienced a moment of the ministry of Jesus, Wonderful Counselor. Jesus met me that day and spoke directly to my heart, unlocking my destiny, unshackling my identity, and restoring my purpose. Like the father in the story of the prodigal son, found in Luke 15:11-31, God met me while I was a long way off. He kissed me, gave me a robe and new shoes, and put a ring on my finger. I still had a calling, an assignment, and authority as His daughter. He still wanted an intimate, personal relationship with me. Incredibly, nothing I'd done disqualified me once God decided I was still His. The beautiful promises from the Father that day gave me something for my mustard seed faith to latch onto. They were an anchor to hold me steady, to keep me from being blown off course, although the wind and the waves never seemed to stop for long.

Hindsight brings some crazy clarity! Rereading my journals from that season, I could see clearly the work God was doing in my life and my family. I began to pray over Jose and the kids. I prayed for unity in our family and prayed a lot to break selfishness. I needed God to continue to rescue us from the mess Jose and I had made, the patterns and mindsets we had taught by example. I remember feeling like the kids were worse behaved than ever. I felt like my home was a war zone, full of manipulation, division, and conflict. What a harvest we were reaping now that we saw our lives in light of the kingdom. I remembered what life was "supposed to be" for Christian families, and I thought that picture was what we were supposed to look like. I would push the kids toward my own image of what we were supposed to act like now that we were church folk, and when they would push back, I would get angry. I was still trying to do things my way and in my own strength. Because of the shame I now know I was dealing with, I see all the ways I was trying so hard to prove I was allowed to be in God's presence.

The way I'd yearned for the leaders of my discipleship program to approve of me and so control the image they saw on the outside was repeating itself with my new church leadership and even with God. I had to learn to surrender my restoration, Jose's restoration, and my kids to Jesus and not force what I wanted for the sake of appearances. I learned to relate to God the Father as a parent and better understood what fatherly love looks like. I read Psalms to learn again how to pray with authenticity. I had to learn how to exchange my strength for His. I poured out my heart as honestly as I could. My heart's desire became to worship in spirit and in truth rather than in my logic and strength or behind a mask of what was "supposed to be." I learned to use Scripture to encourage myself despite the circumstances. I even recorded myself claiming the promises of biblical truth voiced over inspirational movie soundtracks so that I could play it back and allow my spirit and my faith to rise within me.

God is the author of our story and He is always writing redemption and purpose into our lives. Even if we have run far away, when we turn back to Him, He runs to meet us with open arms. There was still much healing to come, but returning to God's presence felt so good and so right. If you're on the precipice of a decision, let my experience help push you over the edge. You too can begin to live as I did, in the truth found in Ephesians 1:3-8:

3 Blessed be the God and Father of our Lord Jesus Christ, who has blessed us in Christ with every spiritual blessing in the heavenly places, 4 even as he chose us in him before the foundation of the world, that we should be holy and blameless before him. In love 5 he predestined us for adoption to himself as sons through Jesus Christ, according to the purpose of his will, 6 to the praise of his glorious grace, with which he has blessed us in the Beloved. 7 In him we have redemption through his blood, the forgiveness of our trespasses, according to the riches of his grace, 8 which he lavished upon us, in all wisdom and insight.

9

FINDING HEALING

Jose and I could never have imagined all the ways God has shown up for us. He has been immensely good, abundantly merciful, eternally forgiving. He gives us so many chances to choose Him. The apostle Paul had some incredible insights into this and he shares with us beautifully in Romans 3:21-25:

'21 But now the righteousness of God has been clearly revealed [independently and completely] apart from the Law, though it is [actually] confirmed by the Law and the [words and writings of the] Prophets. 22 This righteousness of God comes through faith in Jesus Christ for all those [Jew or Gentile] who believe [and trust in Him and acknowledge Him as God's Son]. There is no distinction, 23 since all have sinned and continually fall short of the glory of God, 24 and are being justified [declared free of the guilt of sin, made acceptable to God, and granted eternal life] as a gift by His [precious, undeserved] grace, through the redemption [the payment for our sin] which is [provided] in Christ Jesus, 25 whom God displayed publicly [before the eyes of the world] as a [life-giv-

ing] sacrifice of atonement and reconciliation (propitiation) by His blood [to be received] through faith. This was to demonstrate His righteousness [which demands punishment for sin], because in His forbearance [His deliberate restraint] He passed over the sins previously committed [before Jesus' crucifixion].'

How unbelievable is it that God would look at me, knowing all my mistakes, and choose me? He chose me not for all the things I could do well but for the potential of His glory to be revealed in me and my weaknesses. His plans for me are not to wander through life blind and confused, but if I lean on Him, I can partner with Him and His story. I am qualified and made righteous because it pleases Him to make it so. A phrase used to describe God's grace toward us, His "good pleasure" has no secret hidden meaning in the Greek. *Eudokia* is defined as will, choice, delight, and satisfaction. So God sees me and has set me apart to partner with Jesus as a part of His grander, big-picture plans on earth just because I make Him smile. To put it very simply, He partners with me because He feels like it. That's so wild to consider! I truly have developed a love for the Word of God over the years. It's God's love letter to me, and when I feel lost or feel like God is distant, there is nothing better than having a written record of how He feels about me to refer to. I don't have to wonder or guess what He's saying because He is unchanging, and His Word never fails!

Returning to church, I knew I would have to live the Christian life completely sold out. To use poker terminology, I was going "all in." There would be no going halfway for me this time. As I have said, I started off trying to force my way into doing and saying all the right things, looking "right" to the people around me so they wouldn't see the real me and kick me out again. I had much time to make up so I dove into the Bible. I had to remind myself of who

God was and what the Bible said. The Word came alive to me as it had done all those years before when I was translating Proverbs. That time, that punishment, God later told me, was some of His favorite shared with me. I was completely focused on Him and listening to what His Word meant for me. Coming back to the Word, in pursuit of knowing Him, I was pleasantly reminded of all the good things that I'd learned during the years in the discipleship program. I was reminded of the prophetic words that had been spoken over me as a teenager at my youth group. I was still God's princess. I was His daughter and He was so glad I was home again. He had not withheld anything from me nor disqualified me from His plans. He was just waiting for me to come back to Him.

FIRST SIGNS OF GROWTH

A teaching gift was beginning to grow. I was learning to take the Word of God and break it down so that others could understand the depth of what they had read. I found myself relating the stories and characters to some unconventional things. Praise God for using foolish things to confound the wise. He speaks to each of us in our own language and always knows what will reach us. Some of the coolest conversations I've had with God are based on movie quotes! During these days of renewed biblical exploration, I fell in love with the story of Lazarus in John 11. I was challenged to write down what God was showing me, not just in journals but typed and formatted like a sermon! I have written several sermons based on what God has shown me in the story of Lazarus but one of the earliest and certainly unconventional ones was titled "Don't Be a Zombie." I built on the last verses of the story, John 11:43-44:

43 When he had said this, Jesus called in a loud voice, "Lazarus, come out!" 44 The dead man came out, his hands and feet wrapped with strips of linen, and a cloth around his face. Jesus said to them, "Take off the grave clothes and let him go."

And Proverbs 16:25.
25 There is a way which seems right to a man and appears straight before him, But its end is the way of death.

The gist of the message was that when we depend on our logic and only what makes sense to us, we go through life like a zombie, insatiably seeking brain after brain (logic) to consume. Zombies do not even realize they are dead; they are doomed to wander aimlessly, attempting to fill a void that will never be satisfied. Lazarus had to throw off his burial clothes and accept the gift of resurrected life through the gift of Jesus. We are presented with the same challenge in Hebrews 12:1:

1 Therefore, since we are surrounded by such a great cloud of witnesses, let us throw off everything that hinders and the sin that so easily entangles. And let us run with perseverance the race marked out for us,

And in Romans 12:1- 2:
1 Therefore, I urge you, brothers and sisters, in view of God's mercy, to offer your bodies as a living sacrifice, holy and pleasing to God—this is your true and proper worship. 2 Do not conform to the pattern of this world, but be transformed by the renewing of your mind. Then you will be able to test and approve what God's will is—his good, pleasing and perfect will.

The next time I read through the story of Lazarus, what stood out most was the emotions of Jesus. He knew He was going to resurrect Lazarus and that everything would be okay but there are some moments of real pain that Jesus experiences once He is with this family in their time of mourning. Pretty interesting for someone who knew the end of the story all along. The Bible tells us that Jesus loved Lazarus and his sisters. When He is talking with them about their confusion and grief, we see Jesus frustrated and hurting alongside His friends. Here was the biblical example that served as proof for me that Jesus hurts with me, cries with me, and is troubled on my behalf. He doesn't want to see any of us hurting and even though He knows the end from the beginning and that all will be well, He understands that the process really sucks sometimes. In the story of Lazarus, we see a Savior who wishes our process didn't have to hurt, who is not only empathetic but wise enough to guide us through our pain into a greater knowledge of Him. He doesn't waste our pain. We also see in this story that God's process of answering our prayers is not just for us, but for the people around us we are praying for. The miracles God works in our lives are a testimony for our family and friends who don't know anything about God other than what they see in us!

LEARNING TO FEED ON THE WORD

I was learning about God by seeing Him work in my circumstances. Life was stormy in this season of renewed dedication to Jesus. Jose and I were attempting to reset the culture of who we were and that did not come without opposition. I extrapolated some amazing truths from Jesus, and Peter, walking on the water. The story is found in all the Gospels with varying details based on the perspective and overall message the author was conveying according to the Holy Spirit. It can be found in Matthew 14:22-33, Mark 6:45-51, and John 6:15-21. In Luke 9:18-20 we read the revelation Peter has about who Jesus is after the feeding of the five thousand, which happens right before the storm and the walking on the water account.

18 Once when Jesus was praying in private and his disciples were with him, he asked them, "Who do the crowds say I am?" 19 They replied, "Some say John the Baptist; others say Elijah; and still others, that one of the prophets of long ago has come back to life." 20 "But what about you?" he asked. "Who do you say I am?" Peter answered, "God's Messiah."

Peter was bold enough to step out of the boat because he knew who Jesus is. From the example of this story, we can be confident that Jesus is the one who calms the wind and puts us at our destination. We also see that as He did by calling out Peter, Jesus allows us to be like Him and teaches us how. His presence leaves no room for fear but allows us to face our call with the same confidence that He sends us out. Jesus did not send the storm on the sea to teach the disciples a lesson. The circumstance brought about a teachable moment. This account found in Scripture, regardless of which Gospel you read it out of, is not about making the trip or how to survive to the other side. It's a reminder to KNOW HIM FIRST and to guard your heart from fear and circumstances, keeping it open and receptive even while doing the ministry. All the disciples had been working hard following Jesus and caring for the multitudes, also following along with them. This boat trip was supposed to be a vacation for them, some good, old-fashioned R&R. Because the disciples were focused on the circumstances and their feelings, they quickly forgot about the miracle they had just been a part of in feeding the five thousand. They even had leftover bread and fish in their boat! Only Peter was able to shift his focus onto who Jesus is and, therefore, what was possible in Him despite facing scary circumstances.

I continued to write sermons and thoughts, interesting passages I wanted to go back and study, and I continue even today to fill up my Google Drive folder with ideas and revelations. I challenged myself to read through the entire Bible for the first time and to make notes of the parts that came alive to me. It's a slow way to read with cross-referencing and some back and forth, but it's been an exciting journey. God told me He would anoint my time spent on my laptop and with the Bible. Reading, studying, writing, and teaching will be part of my life moving forward. As I walked out my faith with fear and trembling and conquering insecurities, I didn't always feel like I belonged among God's people, but I fought for God's presence and rooted my life in the Word. The Bible has become life to my bones and breath in my lungs.

Jose and I were no longer just attending church, but we were serving. Our church was a portable church-plant in the early days, as we rented space from a movie theater, a high school auditorium, and even the cafeteria of an elementary school. Setup and teardown happened every Sunday and made for some long days but God was moving in the hearts of our people. I began serving in behind-the-scenes ministries, but my heart was drawn to the worship team. I craved God's presence and I needed to respond to what He was doing in my life. I needed to return my breath to Him in songs of praise and adoration. I auditioned and was accepted as a vocalist. Then, a need arose for a secondary bass guitar player, and I felt compelled by Holy Spirit to mention that I'd known how to play bass many years prior. I picked it back up and learned quickly how to get by on the basics. The joy and fulfillment in my spirit from pouring out my talents, my praise, and my love for God to the accompaniment of music was restored to me. My role at church has changed multiple times over the years, and I've helped out with several departments, but the constant has always been worship. In fact, I was part of the worship experience at the church I grew up in and during the discipleship program. All the troubles I'd brought on myself and all the distance I'd tried to put between God and myself could not void the call on my life or the talent God had given me. It was never about my glory —- I've never been one of the best singers on any of the teams I've been involved in, but there was something that could not be denied in my expression of gratitude back to my heavenly Father. My greatest moments of intense intimacy, deliverance, and healing all center around times of musical worship.

It may not be an earth-shattering revelation to you, but the two pillars of my faith discussed in this chapter, worship and the Word, aren't just important for me but for all believers, whether you are talented in singing or not. The living Word is Jesus. We know Jesus and allow Him to know us when we feast on His word, the Bible.

John 1:1-5 tells us:

1 In the beginning was the Word, and the Word was with God, and the Word was God. 2 He was with God in the beginning. 3 Through him all things were made; without him nothing was made that has been made. 4 In him was life, and that life was the light of all mankind. 5 The light shines in the darkness, and the darkness has not overcome it.

Worship is our response to the knowledge of who Jesus is. It's a lifestyle of gratitude and honor to the Trinity who has rescued, restored, and empowered us to be a part of His grand plan.

Over the next several years, God would continue to blow my mind. Jose and I experienced exponential growth in 2018. Perfection still eludes me, of course, but I can see the threads of the tapestry of our life being woven together. We were moving forward. We would never look back. We are all in.

UNDER NEW MANAGEMENT

In the summer of 2017, God decided to turn up the heat. The founding pastors of our church were called to transition back into the workforce. They had launched a church and brought healing to a motley crew of God's people who were hurting. We needed Jesus and we needed each other. Without their leadership, I could never have faced and accepted the love of the Father or from church people. In due course, the time came to stop licking our wounds and get up to do something. We met our new pastors, who have their own incredible story of being led to Georgia from a thriving church plant in Miami, Florida. One of the first messages I remember hearing from our new Pastor, Manny Rivera, was addressed to our volunteers, whom we call the Dream Team. He said, "Hear the Word, speak the Word, go for it; you're here to solve a problem!" His encouraging, rallying cry to us was and is, "You can do it, you can make it, you're looking good." And with his blessing and encouragement giving fuel to my fire, the next season of my life felt like even more of a roller coaster than it had been so far. Over the next few months, there were extreme highs and lows.

Jose and I began 2018 by stepping into a vacancy to serve as youth pastors. Jose had experience and passion. I had passion. We rebranded the youth as "Imprint," as in God's fingerprints were on us, and we would leave our imprint on the world around us. In the animal kingdom, imprinting refers to a critical time early in an animal's life when it forms attachments and develops a concept of its own identity. We wanted our students to know their identity in Christ, to form a family that had each other's backs, and to know they could impact people around them of all ages just by being who God had created them to be. Our tagline was, "Be Real, Be Passionate, Belong." We were moderately successful, but there were plenty of moments that felt like trudging through thick mud. We'd take a step forward and then two or three steps back. If you've ever served as a youth pastor before, then you'll know what I mean. There was a palpable tension between seeing so much possibility in front of us and not seeing forward progression among the students consistently. You want so much for them but you cannot make the choices for them or their parents. Often you find yourself watching with a broken heart and spending lots of time in prayer. What I learned was that while preparation of the message each week was imperative, the reception of the students was not my responsibility or within my control. The Bible tells us in 1 Corinthians 3:6-9:

6 I planted the seed, Apollos watered it, but God has been making it grow. 7 So neither the one who plants nor the one who waters is anything, but only God, who makes things grow. 8 The one who plants and the one who waters have one purpose, and they will each be rewarded according to their own labor.

And also in Ezekiel 2:4-8:

4 The people to whom I am sending you are obstinate and stubborn. Say to them, 'This is what the Sovereign Lord says.' 5 And whether they listen or fail to listen—for they are a rebellious people—they will know that a prophet has been among them. 6 And you, son of man, do not be afraid of them or their words. Do not be afraid, though briers and thorns are all around you and you live among scorpions. Do not be afraid of what they say or be terrified by them, though they are a rebellious people. 7 You must speak my words to them, whether they listen or fail to listen, for they are rebellious. 8 But you, son of man, listen to what I say to you. Do not rebel like that rebellious people; open your mouth and eat what I give you."

Coming across those scriptures as an answer to my quandaries with student ministry wasn't super comforting, honestly, but it was the encouragement I needed to obey where the Lord had put me. Obedience, despite the circumstances, was huge for me to grab hold of and apply to my own life. My whole life up until that point had been chosen by convenience or by what I wanted to do. I had been the author of where my life would go for so long, even in the early days of being back at church. Learning to follow Jesus according to His plans and design, learning submission meant un-learning years and years of what made sense to me. Imagine a broken bone that was not reset and just healed but was convenient to the body. That bone would be twisted and disjointed, a source of pain, and impossible for it to fulfill its function or potential. It has to be surrendered to a trained professional to be broken again and set properly to heal and resume its designed use and capacity. Now imagine an entire skeleton of these wounded and twisted, disjointed bones. This is how I imagine I presented myself to the Lord when we returned to church. In His mercy and compassion, God took me in and began the process of resetting and realigning me to His design and purpose piece by piece.

One of the tools God used in this process was Family Foundations, International. Founder and Pastor Craig Hill developed a series of seminars called Ancient Paths designed to uproot the lies of the enemy living in our hearts and exchange them with God's truth. The first time I attended an Ancient Paths seminar, it was part of the discipleship program I attended when I first moved to Georgia in the early 2000s, and it was mandatory. As well-intentioned as the seminars are, my first experience with them was absolutely horrific. There is an organized way to host the seminar and move through the curriculum but in my memory, none of that happened the first time. I was in a room pulled to the side with a young adult leader of the discipleship program and was asked to list off the people I'd had premarital sex with. Then, my list was reported to the directors of the discipleship program, who decided the best course of action was to call my mom and have me tell her the list. My mom felt the need to make the boys' parents aware. I was seventeen years old in my first year away from home, just trying to do the right thing and obey my leaders. When I returned home that summer, I had no friends. I hadn't been allowed to contact the boys, and so with no warning, they were outed and certainly no longer wanted anything to do with me. Now my old friends were concerned about the cult I had joined and kept me at a distance for fear that my convictions would be forced on them as well. Needless to say, even fifteen years later, I was not thrilled about going through this process again. There was no way I was going to sit in a room with my pastors and fellow leaders, whom I still didn't feel comfortable around because I didn't feel like I belonged with them, and reveal all my sins for it to be used as ammunition against me.

Ultimately it came down to faith. I trusted God, mostly, and so I chose to trust my pastors. I can't speak for the rest of the team of leaders who all attended this series of seminars but I am so glad I did. They are the kind of thing that you receive in direct proportion to what you put in. My biggest takeaway from that first round of seminars was learning to allow Jesus and His truth to banish shame. I finally began to permit myself to see myself through God's eyes and not my own!

God was not leading me on a special, unique path. Although the outcome of my and Jose's story makes us the exception in most rooms, the process God was taking us through is available to all believers. The Bible tells is that as we pursue Christ we become more like Him. Pastor Manny says it's not about reading the Bible like any other novel, but letting it read you, We must pursue a relationship with God by reading the love letter He provided for us. It's full of His promises and thoughts toward us. It lets us learn about His nature and in light of who He is, we can see who we are meant to be! It's not an easy journey to start or to compete but it is truly the most worthwhile thing a person can do. Nothing else compares to the joy and peace of living in a relationship with the holy and perfect King of All!

Continue to find yourself in my story and be encouraged to surrender the pen, surrender control. You may be holding onto your own way for one of many reasons: fear that no one cares and you're the only one looking out for you, or shame that says you shouldn't bother anyone else because of how little you deserve. Neither of those thought patterns come from your Heavenly Father. He is desperate to reach you, enough to put this book in your hands so you can read about the miracle that happened to someone else and consider what's possible for you and your family.

10

FINDING PURPOSE

Under our new pastors, the time came to relaunch Discover Life Church. We were moving out of the elementary school and into a new facility in a new but close-by community. As a part of the team of leaders, I participated in rewriting the core values, mission, and vision statements of our church. To my amazement, I was an important part of the direction of the church and I was not just invited to be there among church leadership because I was Jose's wife. Pastor Manny had personally offered me a seat at the table because I am called, I am a leader, and because Jose knew if Pastor Manny didn't personally invite me, I would have an even harder time believing I was actually wanted in those meetings. Those early days were so messy, like when a baby is first learning to feed itself. The baby is going to wear a lot of the food, but one day, it'll click, and using a spoon gets easier and easier. Even when we squabbled or needed a bath, our pastors were so patient with us as we grew. Those of us who stayed the course grew quickly in spiritual maturity and together as a family.

In February 2018, Pastor Jim Hennessy came from Trinity Church in Texas to speak at Discover Life Church and meet the team of leaders. Our pastors, Manny and Victoria Rivera, are his spiritual son and daughter, so this was a visit from our esteemed grandfather in the faith! He said, "You'll never find eternal life eating the earth's bread." Discover Life Church pushed hard to follow after Jesus and leave behind convenience and comfort. We met for corporate prayer midweek, naming it something like, "See you at the well." We were putting a draw on God to reveal to us the deep things. We needed to redig the wells of our "fathers" and return to having our needs met by God the Father, removing all the things that had clogged us up over time. We had powerful prayer sessions, believing that God would send us, specifically the castaways. We felt like a motley crew of recovering wounded, the misfits that didn't fit at the typical church. We wanted God to send us the hurting, the smelly, the homeless, the prostitutes —- and it all sounded really good. We prayed that God would make us ready to receive them, love them, and disciple them. I had a powerful impression then that my home would become a place of refuge for those with nowhere to go but up. Perhaps a halfway house or a shelter in the storm for a single mom. Anyone picking themselves back up could find healing and respite under our roof, in safety, and in God's presence. God was faithful to send people our way.

Our house at the time was already pretty full, without much square footage to spare. We had a few young adults crash on our couch for a weekend but nothing major. Then came a horrible telephone call. A family member had been sexually assaulted and was no longer comfortable or safe in their hometown. My house was exactly the place of rescue they needed, but I never dreamed or expected my rescue mission would be to my own family. Jose and I were heartbroken for them, but we gladly opened the doors, moved our kids around to make room, and let them stay until they felt ready to go back home. I prayed hard during that time for a new, bigger home. Ten people living in 1,250 square feet is tight! If this was God's vision for our house, I knew He would provide for us to continue to say "Yes." That promise took years to come to fruition, but when we finally moved into our new home, it was more than I could have hoped for. More on that later.

RESTORING LOST TIME

March blew in like a lion with an invitation to a conference for church pastors hosted at the church Jose and I had been excommunicated from. I was petrified but my pastors assured us they had our backs and they needed us there. We were obedient, trusting both our pastors and God, and with me praying in tongues the whole car ride! The campus was unrecognizable. I soon realized that my fear was unsubstantiated. Most of the people I was afraid to bump into were no longer there or weren't a part of this event. I did, however, see the old youth pastor who had advised me to disappear after Jose and my affair came to light. We were met with hugs, introduced them to our current pastors, and had a brief exchange over a very shy lunch. I kept waiting for the tar and feathers to come leaping at me from behind but they never did. Folks were just happy to see us back in church somewhere. The door opened for Jose to restore some old relationships that he maintains to this day. In that restoration, we began to plan for youth conferences in our county, partnering with other local churches to bring the truth, the power of God, His overwhelming love, and redemption to even more students and young adults than we could each reach in our own efforts. It was a powerful conference, and Jose and I left elated, relieved, and unburdened. However, we began to find that the highs we experienced were usually accompanied by lows. Over the next few weeks, after feeling the triumph of the conference, one of our family vehicles died. The kids would probably still speak fondly of "Gigi," our Ford Expedition. We were so happy to buy her years before for $5000 cash. At the time, we had been driving a company truck, and we were lucky the kids were small, so they could all illegally squish into the backseat! Gigi was a huge blessing and we celebrated that now all our kids could have their own seat *and* a seat belt! That wasn't our first family car, but certainly the first one all the kids remember. There was panic that one vehicle died, but God showed up and sent vehicles and finances our way. Not only did we have the means to get ourselves around comfortably and legally, but we were also able to replace my mother-in-law's car for her. In tandem with the vehicle mess and recovery, one of our daughters was dealing with a bullying situation at school that came to a head. Her grades and self-esteem were at an all-time low. We didn't know how it would turn out, but we decided to find a home-schooling option for her. Miraculously, even though our best option required tuition, it was a much better solution for her. A couple of years later, we were able to pay it off early, well before time for her graduation.

We continued to travel with our pastors. We received prophetic words of promise, and then we'd come home, and I'd wonder if I was truly where I was supposed to be. The highs and lows we lived through spiritually and practically, sometimes within a single day, came in constant, unrelenting waves. We had grown used to dysfunction and it wasn't letting us go easily.

Have you ever been to the ocean? I love the ocean. I love to rest in the waves and let them lift me off the seafloor. One thing I notice is that when a huge wave comes, powerful and wonderful and overtaking, it is immediately followed by a drawing back. The water is sucked out to sea, and rather than floating, I'm dropped to the sea floor, and I stand there waiting for the next wave. Sometimes it takes several minutes before the next big wave. Sometimes the water seems quiet. You can see a pattern in the waves from a distance, but when you're in the water, it feels like a much different story. The best-known consistency in big powerful waves happens during a storm. Then the waves come in quick succession and it may be hard to keep up and keep your head above water. I'm learning the process of God, and being in His presence is so much like the ocean's waves. I would have a powerful good, followed by what felt like a longer period of void, loneliness, bad things happening, and not belonging. While I wanted to stay hungry for God and His presence, it was easier to constantly complain that God was either too much or too little. The waves either lifted me off my feet, surrounding me and overtaking me, or receded so shallowly that I could easily touch the bottom and had stand on my own. I didn't want to do things of my own strength anymore, so I decided just to lie back and float. I surrendered to the waves so that whether high or low, my feet were up and His presence surrounded me. Surrender is a choice, like physically lifting your feet off the ground while wading in the ocean and allowing the waters to hold you up regardless of the actual depth. So in learning to be a leader at my church and serve alongside my pastors, I chose to believe them. I knew my pastors heard from God that I was a needed part of the team. I surrendered to the call instead of fighting it until it made sense to me. With their encouragement, I kept moving forward and remained in God's process. In June of 2018, I led a mission trip with a group of eight students, all young ladies, to Tijuana, Mexico.

We partnered with our sister church, Impact Church, out of Miami, Florida, and joined them at Rancho de Sus Niños in

Tijuana. For the first time, I was in a big leadership role, a youth pastor responsible for eight young ladies on the other side of the continent, and I found myself there without Jose. I was so afraid I would mess something up but we had an incredible trip!

The girls enjoyed themselves and they worked really hard! Some of our construction projects they had for teams to help with were mixing cement by hand and busting up desert ground with pickaxes and shovels to dig irrigation ditches. We also had the opportunity to minister to the children who attended classes on the campus as well as to the community surrounding the mission. We attended home-church meetings and helped collect trash from neighborhoods. I experienced two personal miracles while there. On June 14, 2018, during a worship service, I was delivered from the depression I'd been carrying and medicating since 2006. I remember singing "Raise a Hallelujah" in Spanish and knowing most of what I was saying, partially because I recognized the song. Being away from the comforts of home and singing from a heart set to worship the Lord, even though the lyrics were in a foreign language, I felt the Lord's presence so strongly. It wasn't long before He began to speak —- not a long, complicated message. He simply whispered, "If you want me to, I'll take it." I knew exactly what He meant. My breath caught in my chest with hope and surprise, but of course, I said, "Yes." I'd been carrying this diagnosis, this mind ailment, for so long that it had become just part of who I was. I'd expected always to have to deal with it on some level. As I exhaled, the breath leaving my body felt thick and the lightness and joy I felt in its place was amazing. Our incredible Savior was there with me. His intent was never for me to carry depression or to believe I was less than what He saw in me. God was steadily chipping away at all the reasons I had trouble believing what He said about me and what my pastors saw in me. Sometimes Jesus heals this way.

Sometimes medication is necessary. I want to be careful and clear to say that when it comes to mental health, please be obedient and open that your path to wholeness may include medical professionals as well as faith-based counseling. If you're struggling, seek wise counsel and pray for God's will for your life. Never leave Him out of the solution!

Later in the mission trip in Tijuana, my team of girls and I completed a high ropes course. Obstacles were assembled between fifty and a hundred feet in the air. Participation required harnesses, carabiner clips, helmets, and of course, ropes. Our objective was to progress through the obstacles as a team, climbing higher and higher as we crossed each one. While I loved the adventure, had no issues with heights, and could have quickly completed the course individually or even with a few of the girls, none of that mattered. I found myself changed. I was patient, encouraging, and genuinely invested in getting all our girls through to the finish together. One obstacle had a series of wooden platforms laid out along three cords of rope. As they stretched from one end to the other, the platforms got smaller. Our goal on this particular obstacle was for all the members of the team to be touching the platform at the same time before moving to the next. For the eight of us participating, this was quite a challenge. At one point, we all had only one foot on the platform and sat back, hovering in the air, trusting in the ropes connecting our harnesses to the cord above our heads. The instructors shared with us a significant metaphor. The cord above us was God the Father. The harnesses represented Jesus' blood, and because of that harness, because of the blood of Jesus, we can connect to God the Father through Holy Spirit, the ropes. We hung onto those ropes and threw ourselves wholly into trusting them even as we hung fifty feet or more in the air. The instructors had not seen any team so completely lean into the harnesses and ropes. It was a powerful lesson for our girls that they could and would trust Holy Spirit when others find a different way. It was also a powerful follow-up for me. I could pastor! I was able to lead, guide, encourage, and build up those girls. For some, it was easy; for others, we had to coach them through each step. The team as a whole joined me in cheering on their teammates who had more difficulty. No one was moving forward through the course without the rest. I was incredibly proud of all of them! I could see then that I already had everything I needed to be significant in my calling. There is always room for growth and polishing for sure, and I can see how God has continued to work on my leadership skills since that day, but the first time I was truly confident that I could do well as a pastor and a leader in the church. I knew the next time an opportunity came, as long as I maintained a connection to God the Father through Jesus Christ and Holy Spirit and trusted in my relationship with Him to empower me to move forward, I would find a deep well inside to pull from. Scripture backs that up in 2 Peter 1:3:

3 His divine power has given us everything we need for a godly life through our knowledge of him who called us by his own glory and goodness.

No matter how inadequate we feel, God gives us everything we need to serve other people and make His name known on earth. And it's through His using our story to lead other people to Him that we find healing. God was taking the broken parts of my heart and healing them. He was making everything new. And through this path of healing, He revealed a purpose for my life.

I am so in awe of God and His goodness and mercy. God had every right to disqualify me and He hasn't. Instead, He looks for ways to promote me. My life is a miracle, an example of God's restoration and the power of the gospel. God sees me redeemed because of the cross and has asked me to be an agent of hope to the broken and hurting like I once was. He has put the coal to my lips and a new song in my heart. I am eternal. I am a miracle. Because I am co-laboring with Christ, I carry within me the power and wisdom to effect change in any situation. Instead of putting me off to the side to make room for the real ministers, He continues to answer my prayers and challenge me to pray bigger and more audacious prayers. It is His pleasure to give me the desires of my heart, especially as my desires are renewed and transformed from glory to glory to reflect Jesus.

BUT WAIT, THERE'S MORE

A big prayer that began in 2015 when my mom moved in with us was for a new house, one with more than enough space for everyone to have their own space instead of having to share. I knew God had called Jose and me to have a home that was a haven for people. A place where they were not only welcomed, but safe. I knew God planned for us to be a shelter and a harbor for people who were going through it, but the 1,200-square-foot house we lived in couldn't possibly be the place for this dream to be realized. It was so cramped and cluttered, with barely enough room for the seven of us who were living there. If you've ever purchased a home before, you will know the nightmare it can be. We had an incredible realtor and a market in our favor but our credit was in terrible shape. Before we spoke to an expert, we barreled ahead based on our misunderstanding of how credit scores and debt history work together. By paying some things off and having history removed from our credit report, we accidentally made things worse where our score was concerned! We tried to make the numbers say what they needed to in our own strength. We looked for houses based on what we wanted and there were so many options. We visited several homes, and nothing quite fit. After several months and so much prayer, believing God would provide for what He had called us to, we realigned our hearts not to making something work, but to waiting on the Lord. It was so tough to walk through, with more complications always waiting in the wings, but I will never forget learning to wait on God and trust Him as the provider. I don't worry about money for days on end. I can choose not to stress whether or not we will have what we need because I know if God did it once, in such a miraculous way, He will always do it. His nature is unchanging and His love toward us never ends!

During the time between praying for the house and receiving it, God was still working on Jose and me, getting us ready for the next season. Praise God that He never stops working on us — He never leaves us incomplete or "good enough." In 2018 Jose and I began to learn about biblical generosity and were excited by the idea of being a storehouse for the Kingdom. We made ourselves available for the Lord to bless us with wealth, not for our own benefit but for blessing others and for financing the spreading of the gospel. Visionaries, Pastors, Missionaries, Evangelists, and so on all need finances to complete the plans and dreams that God has given them. Jose and I wanted to be trusted to distribute seed. We received many prophecies confirming what the Lord had ignited in our hearts, and we continue to walk in the steps He lays out for us, knowing that the destination will include our security but will focus on our openness to be used by Him to benefit others. We continued to pursue the opportunities for ministry in counseling and partnering with Family Foundations, International. The more we obeyed, the more we said "Yes" to whatever God had for us, and the more prayers were answered. We changed, grew, and matured.

We blossomed and we were thriving as we got closer and closer to who God has always designed for us to be. God was making promises, giving us our purpose, and in His wisdom, He used problems to prune us. The Bible tells us about pruning in John 15:1-11:

1 "I am the true vine, and my Father is the gardener. 2 He cuts off every branch in me that bears no fruit, while every branch that does bear fruit he prunes so that it will be even more fruitful. 3 You are already clean because of the word I have spoken to you. 4 Remain in me, as I also remain in you. No branch can bear fruit by itself; it must remain in the vine. Neither can you bear fruit unless you remain in me. 5 "I am the vine; you are the branches. If you remain in me and I in you, you will bear much fruit; apart from me you can do nothing. 6 If you do not remain in me, you are like a branch that is thrown away and withers; such branches are picked up, thrown into the fire and burned. 7 If you remain in me and my words remain in you, ask whatever you wish, and it will be done for you. 8 This is to my Father's glory, that you bear much fruit, showing yourselves to be my disciples. 9 "As the Father has loved me, so have I loved you. Now remain in my love. 10 If you keep my commands, you will remain in my love, just as I have kept my Father's commands and remain in his love. 11 I have told you this so that my joy may be in you and that your joy may be complete.

God knows what He's doing and He is trustworthy. He gets rid of the junk you don't need and helps you develop discipline and structure to maximize your potential. This isn't about salvation or punishment for sin — we're already clean, as it says in verse 3. This passage is all about purpose, stewardship, and being good and faithful servants who multiply what they are given. We have to "remain" in Him. We have to do things His way and according to His plans. This isn't designed to crush us but to identify us as belonging to Jesus so that when we succeed, it's not for something as finite and temporary as our fame but rather as part of the infinite glory of God. Love and obedience are the keys to legacy and multiplication. Jesus gave us these keys so that when we are pruned, or when we have to let go of junk, we understand why and we can remain joyful. Verse 11 says it's Jesus' joy in us that makes our joy complete. What a perspective shift!

So as Jose and I grew in the Lord, we indeed experienced some losses. Some things we were grateful that the Lord removed from us, little problems that caused us headaches, habits or relationships we didn't like anyway, but pruning felt entirely different. When things that seemed to be doing well were taken away, sometimes suddenly, I often found myself focusing on the pain of the cut. I have learned to "remain in Him." I can't run and hide from my feelings. Because I am connected to God as my source, when I'm experiencing death, I need to let Him supply life. If I pull away, then nothing I do will have His touch on it, and I will cease to bear fruit trying to do so on my own. So even when I don't understand, I can agree with what God is doing because I trust Him, and because I trust Him and agree with Him, I can tap into His joy when mine is less than complete.

I was watching a travel documentary recently that exemplified this point. Tulip bulbs in the Netherlands are made strong by cutting the bloom off the plant before it reaches its peak. This transfers all the plant's energy to making the healthiest, strongest bulb, which is then sold off for future planting. The focus is not on the one beautiful bloom but on the legacy of the bulb. A strong bulb will create smaller bulbs in the ground as it grows, which can be dug up, separated, and replanted to mature, blossom, germinate, and spread. Healthy bulbs will blossom and multiply every year! What an incredible picture of discipleship. A new believer begins to flourish and grow. They experience pruning, most likely from a delegated authority figure, but instead of getting offended, they stay the course, allowing their faith in God's sovereignty and continued pursuit to produce strength in their inner being. That strong, healthy, mature believer now can reproduce themselves in others, making disciples and leading others from a place of wisdom to create more and more strong, healthy, blossoming believers.

After discovering a plethora of beautiful metaphors like that, I wish I could say that I consistently keep Jesus' joy during my times of pruning. I wish I could tell you that my life is all eternity-minded and at peace with the Lord. I may not start there when life does not match my expectations but praise God, I do get there, and the times of unrest and being out of peace get shorter and less intense! I'm getting faster at claiming the promise of Scripture, like Isaiah 32:18:

18 My people will live in peaceful dwelling places, in secure homes, in undisturbed places of rest.

11

FINDING HOPE

In 2019 Jose and I were climbing a figurative mountain. Life was challenging, but moving forward and upward, getting better and better over time. Our family was experiencing healing and freedom but we felt a shift coming. We had no idea what 2020 held for us. Things were coming together in our faith as a family, in our work, in our place at church, and we were able to serve people in great ways. Though I'd experienced much unrest in my life, I now knew that in Jesus, my home could be a place of rest, peace, and healing. When you are following God and serving Him, He will reveal the plans and purposes He has for your life. When you lean into those plans, accepting God's pruning and submitting to stay in the process, you will experience great joy and fulfillment. Fruit in your life has no choice but to grow when you're abiding in the vine!

2020 began with an air of mystery. On our church leadership team and personally, we were unsure of any specific direction to head in. It almost felt like God was saying, "Hold the line." Jose and I had joined the counseling ministry team at our church, Discover

Freedom, which implemented the Family Foundations method of Jesus, Wonderful Counselor who had made such a change in our own lives. It was incredible to be a part of helping others find that freedom by bringing them into an encounter with Jesus. In February 2020, we had the opportunity to travel to Belgium to teach a church there how to administer this same method to their people. Travel is dear to my heart, and the people there were so hungry for God. It was an amazing trip!

When we came home, we were settling into the new house we had closed on. It was everything we had been praying for. There was more than enough space for our family and more! Finally, after years of waiting and praying, repairing our credit, and saving, we found a place that felt like home. It was perfect; all the tick marks were checked - even a few I'd forgotten that I wanted. When we put in an offer, I was nervous as to whether or not it would be accepted. My realtor friend had outdone herself. The former owner had been praying as well. He wanted ministry to continue in the home, that it would continue to be a place where God was welcomed and celebrated. During the buying process, there were two bids that the owner had to choose from, ours and another buyer. My realtor, a very close friend, advised that we write a letter to the owner so they could connect with us and feel more informed on how to choose between the comparable bids. I poured out my heart. I couldn't help but paint the vision that God had given me for what my home would be. I described our large family and needing space for them, but also my desire to help others. Our home would be a safe harbor for people to rest, heal, and reconnect with Jesus. We dreamed of having a home that could host small groups, a home that we could use for ministry. Jose was nervous that anyone who was anti-Jesus would reject our bid. We both thought it was risky to put ourselves out there but there were no other words that could have been said.

It was in God's hands now. When we met the former owner at closing, he mentioned the letter. When it arrived in his email inbox, he was driving and praying over who would buy the home. He had to pull to the side of the road, being brought to tears of thankfulness that his prayers were also being answered! God showed Himself faithful to both of us!

Shortly after we moved into our new, prophetic, God-sent home, Covid-19 and all the fear that came with a rapidly spreading and deadly virus brought disruption and confusion to the entire world. Jose, like everyone, was working from home, the kids were attending school online from home, and we had plenty of time to get unpacked and settled. It was actually enjoyable for a while there. Then like so many others, Jose lost his job. In light of the state of the country and businesses downsizing everywhere, companies were reluctant to take on new projects. The expansion into larger markets was no longer getting the traction it once had and so Jose's company decided not to expand at all. They needed to stay focused on the parts of the company that were still working. Unfortunately, that left no role for Jose to stay on with them, and he was let go. Our first thoughts, surprisingly, were good ones; we were excited to see how God would open another stream of revenue into our lives since He was our provider, not any job or company. We had entrusted our lives to Him, not the employer. Several months went by before Jose found another job.

I kept busy volunteering and ministering at the church but I never volunteered to work myself, and Jose never asked me to go to work. I'd only be able to acquire an entry-level position somewhere that wouldn't be near enough to cover our expenses, and we just knew that a job for Jose would come along any day. The problem he ran into was that most places thought Jose was overqualified, and no one was hiring for executive-level positions as he had at his previous job. It was very frustrating but we leaned again on the Lord to be our source and guide our steps. A job finally came along in 2021 paying much less than he had been making but it was a good job helping other faith-based startups. Jose had the opportunity to pray and minister to loads of people.

ANCHORED THROUGH CONTINUED STORMS

Our family seemed to be managing the stress of it all fairly well. We had our three teenage daughters still at home, one son in his twenties, my mother, and Jose's sister and her son had moved in. She also had been sent to work from home, had recently sold her home, and needed a temporary place to get her bearings while the world and the housing market settled down. Jose and I were more committed to each other than ever before. We spent time to honestly and vulnerably talk to each other, which wasn't always easy with such a full house. I was able to support him and encourage him through the stress he felt as the provider. He supported me and encouraged me that I was needed and helpful and not a burden to him! It was almost like the early days of understanding one another and sharing dreams for the future. Despite everything constantly swirling around us, we were anchored to each other and Christ. Over the years of growth and maturing, we learned much about covenant marriage. The question would come in occasionally if I had done the right thing by staying with Jose, especially when we had money problems. The answer to why I stay with Jose and why he stays with me has nothing to do with either one of our merits and everything to do with trusting God. I know that God honors the covenant, and despite our past, Jose and I are in covenant now. We are a three-stranded cord: Jose, me, and Jesus. His commitment to us is to keep us in the process of becoming, so when I fall short, Jesus will help me. When Jose falls short, Jesus will help him. There is no exit clause; we are in covenant forever, committed to becoming the perfect partner for each other. We are learning to find beauty amid chaos and problems and allowing that beauty to draw us closer to each other and Jesus.

Church had moved to online services only and we sought ways to stay connected. Zoom and FaceTime were incredibly useful for meetings and small groups. We emailed a lot. We called even more. Our church had a daily prayer call and we encouraged all congregants to join for an hour in the morning. We even had a weekly show that we streamed live just to be a little silly and foster connection. The leadership team had to flex and stretch. We had to learn new skills. It took hard work to keep a digital eye on our sheep. As a team, we were very connected and close. There were so many changes and shifts, so many landmines we had to navigate around, but we made it. Eventually, the spread of Covid-19 leveled out, and when new cases finally began to decrease, the world's doors began to open again. We met for church in our new facility wearing masks and were so happy to see each other in person again. There was so much fear and paranoia. People were still scared. The good news was that God was still on the throne — He was still good and as a church, we were going to continue to pursue His face. The rules of how we could do that changed sometimes daily. We had to juggle plans based on who was sick or quarantining. But God's grace was with us. It was a weird time, full of uncertainty, but we leaned heavily on our everlasting Father and put our faith in Him to see us through it.

Going back to John 15, abiding in the vine, there's an incredible promise for us.

12 My command is this: Love each other as I have loved you. 13 Greater love has no one than this: to lay down one's life for one's friends. 14 You are my friends if you do what I command. 15 I no longer call you servants, because a servant does not know his master's business. Instead, I have called you friends, for everything that I learned from my Father I have made known to you. 16 You did not choose me, but I chose you and appointed you so that you might go and bear fruit—fruit that will last—and so that whatever you ask in my name the Father will give you. 17 This is my command: Love each other.

Life was a swirling sea but we were moored to our church and our family to get us through it. We focused on God and love. The most comforting reminder during those days, and honestly any day, is right there in verse sixteen. God chose us and appointed us to bear lasting fruit. When we partner with Him, there is power in our prayers, our words, our hugs. If you're trying to live life in God alone, you will not reach the depths or heights of all God has planned for you. You need people, as frightening as that can be, to walk with you shoulder-to-shoulder and arm-in-arm. As a church family, we pointed each other back to Jesus because nothing else was stable. He held us all together. We were just treading water again —- when another huge storm hit.

12

FINDING GRACE

In March of 2021, my fifteen-year-old daughter and I had a very surprising doctor's appointment. She had been nauseated at what seemed to be random times of day, regardless of what she ate or her activity level. Her COVID tests were all coming back negative, and most of the time, she felt just fine. She'd be sitting at the kitchen table, logged in to her online classes, working on finishing the eighth grade. Then she'd suddenly be gagging, covering her mouth, and trying to make it to the bathroom. Normally, my radar for such things is running well, but I was totally unprepared to hear what we did from the doctor after a "routine" pregnancy test. I remember on the way to the doctor's office, I even told my daughter that they'd most likely do a urine test because she had passed puberty and was experiencing nausea. When they mentioned the test, I nodded along, thinking, "Yep, I knew they would do that." I failed to see the panic on my daughter's face. I'm sure you already suspect what I heard. My baby girl was pregnant. The doctor gave us some time alone and we had a good talk in the office. Of course, at that point, my daughter told me everything she'd been up to in the past year or so. The baby's father was the son of a close family friend, and having sex had been a mutual decision based mostly on boredom. She decided on her own to go through with the pregnancy and determine the details of what that would look like one day at a time. Things could have been much worse, but how would we tell Jose? While the life change we had experienced in recent years was powerful and real, there was hesitancy because of how we, as a family, used to handle bad news. I promised my daughter that I would be with her when we told her dad and that we should do it right away. Jose was incredible. We were both shocked and our emotions ranged all over as we processed the news, but the message we gave our daughter was that we still loved her and we were there to support her through the consequences of her actions. As you read in previous chapters, Jose and I were no strangers to making mistakes. Thankfully, in this case, we were both empowered by Holy Spirit to show grace and mercy. Our first call was to our pastors. I cried over the phone, "What are we gonna do?" They were so gracious and loving. The decision to engage in premarital sex was wrong for sure but they were so proud that we had supported our daughter's decision to keep the baby. My daughter never had to walk through anything alone. She and the young man repented for their bad decision, they owned their choice, and they rededicated their lives to God's purposes for them. Our pastors guided us and led us through some difficult conversations but both sets of parents applauded our teenagers for choosing life. Our entire church became a place of love and support for them and for the four new grandparents too! None of us were ready for something like this and had no idea how to move forward. We knew better how we didn't want to respond and wounds we wanted to prevent. A big question we all asked God was about generational curses. All four of us grandparents had sinned in promiscuity and had dealt with lust, but we had taken a stand to stop the line of destruction in our families. Had we missed something that allowed our kids to fall the same way we did? God very gently answered the question for all four of us in different ways but He gave us all the same answer. We *had* drawn a line in the sand; we *had* set our kids up to succeed and make the right choices. The key word there is *choice*. Free will is God-given to every person, and although the setup was made for the contrary, the wrong choice was made. What God pointed out to us that our children and our grandchild escaped was the judgment, the whispers, being tossed aside or written off. They were not shunned or forced into marrying each other. They were never forgotten or alone. Yes, some tough conversations and changes had to be made. But even in the hard parts, they only knew mercy, love, support, and forgiveness. We spoke life to them, reaffirmed their purpose and call, their identity in the Lord. It's been two years since our granddaughter was born, and there has been so much growth in the lives of these two teenagers. They are accomplished students, mature believers, and really good parents. Our granddaughter is the happiest, sweetest little baby. As time goes by, I have full confidence that all three of them will achieve all that God has for them. I know that as long as they keep Jesus at the center of their lives, then it will be impossible for them to fail. And because we were obedient to show God's love and mercy to them, none of us grandparents will miss any moment of it. We will be there to help them navigate their futures as parents and individuals.

THE ANCHOR HOLDS

No matter what circumstances have been thrown at us so far, God has shown Himself faithful to protect and fight for us and to rewrite our messy narratives to match His design. My daughter and I have been able to share our story, her story, with other young moms and a local ministry that partners a life-affirming medical clinic with faith-based resources for low-income families. When you are surrounded by people who want to reflect the love and grace of Christ, the community you build can withstand any hardship and come out stronger because of it. I was amazed and so grateful for the way the community came around my daughter. My own sin and pregnancy had been under very different circumstances, but I'd not experienced the acceptance, grace, and support that I saw being extended to my daughter. I was so thankful that the cycle of hurt and rejection was not being repeated in her life. God again, was proving Himself faithful to us. Psalm 103:17 says,

17 But from everlasting to everlasting the Lord's love is with those who fear him, and his righteousness with their children's children.

He was keeping us all safe and had more for us than we had yet touched but we had to stay the course to get there. I can admit it was easy to retreat into the bubble of "being there" for my daughter, and I'm grateful that I was able to. Over time it was becoming obvious that I would not stay much longer in the bubble, that I couldn't use circumstances to hide from my calling. God had more for me and I needed to get ready.

13
FINDING COMMUNITY

Isaiah 61:7-9 says:

7 Instead of your shame you will receive a double portion, and instead of disgrace you will rejoice in your inheritance. And so you will inherit a double portion in your land, and everlasting joy will be yours. 8 "For I, the Lord, love justice; I hate robbery and wrongdoing. In my faithfulness I will reward my people and make an everlasting covenant with them. 9 Their descendants will be known among the nations and their offspring among the peoples. All who see them will acknowledge that they are a people the Lord has blessed."

I cannot tell this story and leave out the best part. One of the prayers that our family shared was that Jose's ex-wife, Robin, would find a relationship with God. Spoiler alert, God answers prayers in miraculous ways we could never imagine!

In less than three years from the time Jose and I returned to church in Easter of 2015, God had done a miracle in our lives and for our kids, and I saw it first in the heart adjustment in me. Our children, rather than being just another divorce statistic, have four parents who love them. More than just being civil, we can actually spend time together. Even our holiday traditions have changed to include time with all of us together. We can enjoy each other's company sincerely and nobody else has to get it.

It began when a guest speaker shared at Discover Life Church and taught us the real meaning of heaping hot coals on someone's head. It's not sneaky vengeance but giving out life! People came to the center of the village to get coal from a constantly tendered fire. They took that coal, carried in a pot on their heads, to their homes to cook with and provide light and warmth, keeping their individual hearths lit. When you heap hot coals on someone's head, you are giving from what could be yours to give someone else life. Praying for your enemies does just that.

When our daughters would ask whether or not Mommy knew Jesus and if she could come to church with us, the best answer Jose and I could give was to pray for her. The Lord convicted me not just to instruct my young daughters to pray but to teach them how. That meant I would be joining them in praying for their mom. Then, God upped the ante and kept bringing Robin to mind asking me to pray for her. I did not want to pray for my husband's ex-wife. I wanted the best for her so she would leave us in peace, sure. I wanted her best so she could be a good mom to her daughters, sure. But if she came to the same church as us, I would surely lose many of the connections I'd made. Surely people would take sides or feel sorry for her. The way they saw me would change. It was scary to invite the possibility of rejection into what had become a place of safety. To be completely honest, even without Robin being there, I still battled with insecurity and a sense of belonging. I often felt like a phony who would be soon found out. Robin was just another easy scapegoat for those insecurities. Nevertheless, I prayed. I prayed with my daughters and I prayed without them. They were not heaven-rending prayers of power and passion, but they did change over time. Where they began very simply for God to bless her and bring her home, to any church home, they changed to truly want her to know Jesus and to find joy again.

Before I noticed any change in Robin, I noticed a change in me. That change made room for unity. My heart was open to her. I remember praying for her and her now husband, Tery, while they were dating. I remember she was so hopeful and nervous, and I remember feeling compassion for her. I wanted her to have a fairy tale love story and to feel swept off her feet. I wanted Tery to be good for her and for her to be loved like she truly deserved to be loved. Could she have stomped on my intentions and heart and made me regret it all and say to God, "See? I knew this would go badly…" Maybe, but I trusted that if God could change my heart, then He could help Robin too. I could trust God to take care of me and Jose, of Robin and Tery, and the kids and I didn't need to understand how all the pieces would land. I just needed to keep praying. Unbeknownst to me and Jose, Robin was also praying and making room for God to work in her life and Tery's life. Because we all said yes to getting out of the way and letting God work on us, my family has experienced a miracle. No family that was as messy as ours was before Jesus could ever come together as we have in such a short amount of time without a miracle!

If you had told me years ago that one day, Robin and I would be friends, I would have laughed in your face. Actually, no—I would have *rolled my eyes* and walked away.

Robin was José's ex-wife. I was the other woman. I had stepped into her children's lives in a role that wasn't mine to take, and there were moments when they enjoyed my company **too much**. It created tension. Rightfully so. By all accounts, we should have been enemies. Tery, her husband, should have sided with her. At best, he should have been neutral. Instead, because of Jesus, **we became family**.

It makes no sense. None of it does. But that's what grace does—it takes the impossible and makes it a reality. It rewrites what *should have been* into what *only God could do.*

CHANGED HEARTS MAKE NEW RIPPLES

It's now been seven years and the fruit on our family tree is absolutely an incredible sight! Jose and I have six children together and two granddaughters. Four of those six and one grandchild we share biologically with Robin, and her husband, Tery, has two children of his own. Of those ten children, six have made their own decisions to follow Christ or rededicate their lives to Him. Six attend services regularly with us, and an additional daughter would if she lived closer. Three of the girls are serving in several ministry teams at the church, including Kids' Ministry, Photography, Worship, and our Cafe. One is helping launch our new Prophetic Dance team. One is about to go on her third overseas mission trip. One has changed her future life plans to be in full-time ministry and is part of our ministry training school. We continue to pray for the remaining four sons who are searching but not settled.

Our family is serving God together. I've mentioned that Jose and I are part of the leadership team at our church; well, so are Robin and Tery. Robin is Director of Nursery and Early Childcare and Tery is a vital part of our Security and Ushers Team. We dog-sit each other's fur babies, spend game nights and holidays together, and even have a blended family vacation planned for the fall of 2023. Robin and Tery are two of our closest friends. And trust me, as strange as that may be to read, it's strange to write. I would never have dreamed that God's restoration would look like this, even three years ago when we were just getting started and still trying to figure out what following Jesus was going to look like. Now, when I tell our story, it's not as a warning or a disclaimer to people, letting them know who I am before they hear it from someone else. No, it's a truthful account of the amazing things God can do.

Our story is one of hope and life to others, especially in a society where divorce and blended families are so common. The verse from Isaiah 61 at the beginning of this chapter is our blended family verse. It's the promise we are standing on and it's who we are. It's a reminder not only of what God has done but what He has promised through a covenant with us to continue to do. Covenants aren't like contracts. It's not a 'if-you-do-then-I-will' kind of agreement. A covenant says because I am, I will.

We have not only seen evidence of this family covenant in our marriages and our kids. It extends! My parents had divorced when I was six due to infidelity, but are now reconciled and spending their old age caring for each other. Thirty-two years of animosity and unforgiveness melted away because they had a few really good conversations. What!? That doesn't just happen! My mother-in-law, diagnosed with cancer for the sixth time, was told that it had spread throughout her body, but it had stopped growing for now. The doctors told her they couldn't get rid of all of it, and whenever it decided to grow again, her life would end quickly. Until then, keep coming in for scans and live your life. On her last scan, after a lifestyle of prayer and faith in the miraculous healing power of Jesus, there was NO sign of any cancer anywhere in her body! That doesn't just happen. Our nieces and nephews are making decisions for Christ and growing in their relationships with God. They are leaders in their jobs, classes, and peer groups. Are any of us perfect? Of course not. Did revival spread to our entire family? Not yet, but we keep praying and believing God's promises. Consider the passage below, the salvation of the Philippian jailer in Acts 16:25-34:

25 About midnight Paul and Silas were praying and singing hymns to God, and the prisoners were listening to them, 26 and suddenly there was a great earthquake, so that the foundations of the prison were shaken. And immediately all the doors were opened, and everyone's bonds were unfastened. 27 When the jailer woke and saw that the prison doors were open, he drew his sword and was about to kill himself, supposing that the prisoners had escaped. 28 But Paul cried with a loud voice, "Do not harm yourself, for we are all here." 29 And the jailer called for lights and rushed in, and trembling with fear he fell down before Paul and Silas. 30 Then he brought them out and said, "Sirs, what must I do to be saved?" 31 And they said, "Believe in the Lord Jesus, and you will be saved, you and your household." 32 And they spoke the word of the Lord to him and to all who were in his house. 33 And he took them the same hour of the night and washed their wounds; and he was baptized at once, he and all his family. 34 Then he brought them up into his house and set food before them. And he rejoiced along with his entire household that he had believed in God.

Paul and Silas were at a really low point in their ministry. They had just exorcized demons from a young girl who had been making the city leaders lots of money as a fortune teller. So they were beaten again, arrested again, and jailed again. They were shackled in the bottom of the jail where all the sewage gathered and assuredly was actively infecting their open wounds. They were not complaining or even just trying to recover or sleep. They were praying and worshiping God and the other prisoners listened without heckling. When the power of God manifested on their behalf, they didn't use it to take advantage of the situation but remained in jail. They knew the Author of their story had put them in that jail for a reason. All the prisoners were set free. More incredible than that, the jailer *and his household* heard the gospel, believed in the Lord, and were baptized. The book of Philippians is a letter Paul wrote later in his ministry to the church, likely founded in part by this same jailer and his family!

God's promises to us are not just for us but for those around us to see. Those closest to us cannot help but notice the changes in our lives from who we used to be. Our story is being written so that it points not to what good people we are but to what God can do, even with very little. I know that Jesus loves our family. I know that we are walking in favor, but it's not because of anything we earned. Our response to God's mercy in our lives can only be our best attempt to remain in right standing with Him. There's no checklist for that. It's maintained by cultivating a deep, real, personal relationship with the Creator of Heaven and Earth, who loves me so much that He died for the chance that I might say yes to Him. My name is tattooed in the palm of His hand and He rejoices over me with singing. Why wouldn't I do all I could to keep Jesus first and central to everything I do? Because that is my heart's desire and God's will, then everything else I could possibly need is already mine. From that heart posture, all my prayers are in alignment with God's will, so the answer is "Yes."

Psalm 37:4 says:

4 Delight yourself in the Lord and He will give you the de-
sires of your heart.

And Jesus tells us in Matthew 6:25-33:

25 "Therefore I tell you, do not worry about your life, what you
will eat or drink; or about your body, what you will wear. Is not life
more than food, and the body more than clothes? 26 Look at the birds
of the air; they do not sow or reap or store away in barns, and yet your
heavenly Father feeds them. Are you not much more valuable than
they? 27 Can any one of you by worrying add a single hour to your life?
28 "And why do you worry about clothes? See how the flowers of the
field grow. They do not labor or spin. 29 Yet I tell you that not even
Solomon in all his splendor was dressed like one of these. 30 If that is
how God clothes the grass of the field, which is here today and tomor-
row is thrown into the fire, will he not much more clothe you—you of
little faith? 31 So do not worry, saying, 'What shall we eat?' or 'What
shall we drink?' or 'What shall we wear?' 32 For the pagans run after
all these things, and your heavenly Father knows that you need them.
33 But seek first his kingdom and his righteousness, and all these things
will be given to you as well.

Jesus, my Savior, my Healer, my Friend. I am so blown away by
your goodness. I cannot believe the words written on these pages.
My heart bursts with gratitude beyond words. My heart's cry is to
stay focused on you, first and central. Nothing else is worthwhile!
I never imagined that the pain I experienced in my youth could be
healed and transformed so completely, but God took my story and
my pain and brought community to help heal the wounds.

14

MY STORY ISN'T OVER

So what now? What else can we pile on the top of this unbelievable story? What else could we have to go through? Well, I'm
not in heaven yet, so there has to be more for me. My pastor often
preaches on capacity building — how God makes room for the
gifts He gives. The process is certainly not fun or easy but the fruit
it yields is well worth the pain in getting there. It's said best in
James 1:2-5:

> *2 Consider it pure joy, my brothers and sisters, whenever you face
> trials of many kinds, 3 because you know that the testing of your
> faith produces perseverance. 4 Let perseverance finish its work so
> that you may be mature and complete, not lacking anything. 5 If
> any of you lacks wisdom, you should ask God, who gives generously
> to all without finding fault, and it will be given to you.*

There's so much to dissect in this passage! *Whenever,* not *if,* you face trials. Trials of many kinds. Perseverance is finished with us when we lack nothing. Until then, buckle up, buttercup! But there's hope even before the finish line. Verse five tells us that when we don't know what to do, we can ask God, who gives generously without finding fault! He doesn't look for a reason not to help, God promises to come through! The plan from the moment of creation, when God already knew that we would make a mess of His storyline for us, was not only to provide us a way back into righteousness through Jesus' death on the cross as atonement for our sin but so much more through His resurrection. In John 16:12-15 Jesus says:

12 "I have much more to say to you, more than you can now bear. 13 But when he, the Spirit of truth, comes, he will guide you into all the truth. He will not speak on his own; he will speak only what he hears, and he will tell you what is yet to come. 14 He will glorify me because it is from me that he will receive what he will make known to you. 15 All that belongs to the Father is mine. That is why I said the Spirit will receive from me what he will make known to you."

In John 14:26-27 He says again:

26 But the Advocate, the Holy Spirit, whom the Father will send in my name, will teach you all things and will remind you of everything I have said to you. 27 Peace I leave with you; my peace I give you. I do not give to you as the world gives. Do not let your hearts be troubled and do not be afraid.

Holy Spirit, the third member of the Trinity, can live inside you and help you, comfort you in the painful parts of the process, and remind you of what you've learned. You don't have to feel lost in the woods between where you are now and your next step. You have the answer to every problem you could come across. From way back in the book of Exodus, God has identified Himself as "I AM" and we can fill in the blank behind that with whatever it is we need in the storyline He is writing for us. We can trust Him and lean on Him. He will never leave us or forsake us. No matter what plans we write, no matter the enemy's schemes, no matter what's written for us by other people, God is The Author. He has the final say. He gets the last word and the final rewrite.

Paul tells us in Romans 8:18-31:

18 I consider that our present sufferings are not worth comparing with the glory that will be revealed in us. 19 For the creation waits in eager expectation for the children of God to be revealed. 20 For the creation was subjected to frustration, not by its own choice, but by the will of the one who subjected it, in hope 21 that the creation itself will be liberated from its bondage to decay and brought into the freedom and glory of the children of God. 22 We know that the whole creation has been groaning as in the pains of childbirth right up to the present time.

23 Not only so, but we ourselves, who have the firstfruits of the Spirit, groan inwardly as we wait eagerly for our adoption to sonship, the redemption of our bodies. 24 For in this hope we were saved. But hope that is seen is no hope at all. Who hopes for what they already have? 25 But if we hope for what we do not yet have, we wait for it patiently. 26 In the same way, the Spirit helps us in our weakness. We do not know what we ought to pray for, but the Spirit himself intercedes for us through wordless groans. 27 And he who searches our hearts knows the mind of the Spirit, because the Spirit intercedes for God's people in accordance with the will of God. 28 And we know that in all things God works for the good of those who love him, who have been called according to his purpose. 29 For those God foreknew he also predestined to be conformed to the image of his Son, that he might be the firstborn among many brothers and sisters. 30 And those he predestined, he also called; those he called, he also justified; those he justified, he also glorified. 31 What, then, shall we say in response to these things? If God is for us, who can be against us?

REMEMBERING WHAT I'VE LEARNED

I aim to trust in the Lord, empowered by the Holy Spirit to hope, whenever I am facing trials of many kinds. I ask Him to remind me what His best looks like and exchange my plans to fix things for doing things God's way. For example, that house of promise we were blessed to move into back in February 2020? The time came in February 2023, a short three years later, to sell it. It took a very specific prophetic word and foreclosure warning letters before we aligned ourselves with God's nudging, but we did, in fact, finally line up. We were kicking and screaming on the inside and confused about why God would take away the blessing He had promised just a few years prior. What's ironic is that even though my husband and I are both staff pastors, licensed ministers, counselors, and so on, our very practical, business-minded brother had the right perspective even before we did.

When told the news about our deciding to sell the big house and downsize he said, "Wow, God really loves you guys." Jose and I were shocked. How could he say that? We certainly didn't feel loved by God. We felt punished, like somewhere along the line, we didn't steward something correctly, and now it was being taken from us, like the wicked servant who had buried his one talent.

The truth of the matter was that God was trying to open another door of provision for us but Jose and I were once again stuck trying to do things our way because our way made the most sense to us. We needed income much more than what Jose was bringing in, and more than just my getting a job would have helped. We needed a major change. I was not opposed to going back to work this time, but I was concerned about losing my time at the church and running the home. A cousin who has owned his own business for more than two decades had talked with Jose in the past about working with him in the past but the timing just wasn't ever right. The door opened for both of us to begin working with our cousin in the summer of 2022, and in just a few months, our bank statements were looking vastly improved. Our credit cards were still maxed out but we had enough to keep the lights on and food on the table with the promise of more work on the horizon, but we were fighting for ways to stay in the incredible house God had given us. It had only been a few years and in our mind, this was supposed to be a long-term home. Because of the COVID-19 global pandemic, many, many people had to choose forbearance arrangements for their mortgages, and we made that choice too. Now that the time of forbearance was ending, the bank wanted more than double what the monthly mortgage payment had been. Try as we might to make the numbers stretch, it just wasn't happening. The math wasn't "mathing." So we surrendered and met with a realtor.

Incredibly, in the few years since we bought the house, its value had greatly increased. As we shared with our brother our plans to sell and went over the prospective numbers he was able to point out what we couldn't see. "How else can you explain living in such a fabulous house for three years, for free, helping house two other families when they had nowhere to go, keeping an open door for young men and women looking for comfort and counsel, taking care of your daughter and her baby, making room for everyone who needed it and then being in a position to sell for a profit!" Our brother continued, "You guys give so much, and God absolutely loves and takes care of you for it. The way you guys live doesn't always make sense to me, but when stuff like this happens, you can't deny that God takes care of His people." Wow! What an incredible shift of perspective. And what a testimony for God's glory! Paul expresses this sentiment in Philippians 1: 12-14 (Amplified)

12 Now I want you to know, believers, that what has happened to me [this imprisonment that was meant to stop me] has actually served to advance [the spread of] the good news [regarding salvation]. 13 My imprisonment in [the cause of] Christ has become common knowledge throughout the whole praetorian (imperial) guard and to everyone else. 14 Because of my chains [seeing that I am doing well and that God is accomplishing great things], most of the brothers have renewed confidence in the Lord, and have far more courage to speak the word of God [concerning salvation] without fear [of the consequences, seeing that God can work His good in all circumstances].

COMFORT DESPITE MYSTERY

Jose and I, at the moment, are a bit like Abram, instructed by the Lord to leave our family, our place of comfort, to go to the land He will show us. I do not know exactly what the Lord has for us next. I have written down, recorded, and saved the plethora of prophecies we have received over the years, and I know the gifting that resides in us, but we can only see through the glass dimly. I know Who is writing my story. Somewhere along the way, I am finally able to refuse to take the pen for myself or to give it away flippantly to anyone ever again. I trust the Author.

I've learned there's a difference between running from negative thinking and truly disarming the liar. The latter requires dependence on God to reveal what's happening in the heart. It requires obedience and vulnerability to allow Him to look and then even more obedience to allow Him to show us what He wants to do to create change, exchanging lies for God's truth. It's my choice whether or not I am empowered by His truth, grace, and mercy or if I decide instead to wallow in negativity, waiting for it to somehow go away on its own.

I have not written this book from a place of consistent victory. Sometimes I wrote from the mountaintop, and sometimes from the valley. In the time to put this book together, my life has had seasons. No matter what my circumstances, whether it be the heights of breakthroughs or the lows of revisiting the past hurts, I want what comes out of me to glorify God. I am not closing my eyes to life happening around me and just believing it will work out. I am standing firm on God's promises and His very nature. I am encouraging myself in what He has done for me already to increase my faith to believe in what He is doing now. I know that even when I don't understand, even when I'm scared, and even when it hurts, God is working for my good. I can trust Him no matter what happens to me on this temporary Earth. I can trust that what really matters, what's gold, will remain. I consistently pray that God removes from my life anything that is in His way, anything I don't need to hang onto. How can I panic or get angry when the "trouble" I'm facing may be God answering my prayers? I'm in a constant battle to trust God in all things, to lean into His principles and the knowledge I have learned over the years of this incredible life I have lived. And I'm still young! The road in front of me stretches out far into the distance. I have to remember to ask for the wisdom to apply what I have learned, not just collect knowledge.

WHO'S HOLDING YOUR PEN?

Maybe you, too, know the struggle of moving information from your head to your heart. Maybe you long to transition from a theoretical perspective of Jesus to know Him in and through you as completely as you know the sun will rise. I pray that you are encouraged and that your faith strengthens for the journey.

If you have missed the mark in your journey of life in Christ, know that God can and will always restore you. Don't be lazy or sloppy with His mercy and grace, saying my sin is okay because God will restore me. Be careful not to miss it. Be bold and fearless to do what God has called you to do. Don't waste time with doubt, insecurity, or excuses. You have everything in Christ that you need to succeed in godliness. Run empowered by Holy Spirit and trust that God has your best in His plans.

If Jesus is not your Lord and Savior, if you don't live in a relationship with Him, then first of all, I'm surprised you read this entire book! I can only imagine the hunger in your heart for life to offer something different than it has so far. There must be a yearning deep inside for more. I promise you, God is the answer.

We are all adulterers. We all neglect the things of God to chase after our own happiness and our own plans. We cheapen the eternal and instead cry out for the satisfaction of our temporary ailments. We are Esau, Sarah, and the prodigal son. We are Gomer, and God is Hosea, ever willing to rescue us from prostitution and bring us back home to belong to Him. We just have to have the guts to surrender.

Pray this simple prayer with me:

"Jesus, I know that I'm a sinner. I've not followed your plans for my life. I accept your sacrifice, the price you paid on the cross because I could never make up for what I've done. I believe you have forgiven me. Wash me of my sins and make me brand new. The past is gone and my life is yours. I'm done being in charge. I don't want to write the story of my life anymore. Take the pen, rewrite my story. Let my life from this day forward point others to you and reveal your glory. Amen."

If you prayed that prayer, please email me at Laura@discover-lifeatl.com.

Let's celebrate together and get you connected to some leaders who can help you grow!

REWRITTEN

15

THE RIPPLES CONTINUE TO EXPAND

It has been eight months since I first published this book. In that time, I've wrestled with whether I should make changes—add more details, refine my words, share more of what God has done. But when I step back and truly reflect, the only thing I want to add is this: **All glory belongs to God.**

Eight months ago, we were still praying—crying out—for our sons and daughter-in-law to come to faith in Jesus. We needed another miracle. Another impossibility turned possible. They had seen the worst of us, lived through the mess we had made, and carried wounds from the past that only God could heal. But over time, they began to soften. They watched as José and I changed—not for a moment, not temporarily, but truly. They saw that our relationship with Jesus was real, that we weren't just caught up in emotion or chasing after a phase. They saw the way we responded to trials differently than we had before. They witnessed the transformation in our marriage, in our friendships—especially with Robin and Tery.

And they saw, maybe for the first time, an authentic, imperfect, but undeniable example of what life in Jesus could be. Now, all three of our daughters still serve faithfully in the ministry at our local church. Our daughter-in-law and all three of our sons have made their own decisions to follow Christ and are also all serving together in our local church. We have the pleasure and honor to see them grow in the Lord as we saw them grow from children to adults.

When I first published this book, only one of our daughters had committed to the two-year discipleship program at our church. She has since graduated, and now, the rest of our children are either currently enrolled or planning to join in the next semesters. They understand what it means to be planted, to give their time and talents as an act of worship, and they are hungry—*hungry*—to live fully devoted lives for Christ.

They each had their own journey to get here, their own battles to fight. But they got here. **We are beyond blessed.**

All our children are safe in the ark. Our family, once fractured and lost, has been restored to unity and strength. *Isaiah 61 is about our family—all of us!*

And still, the journey continues.

Jose and I still feel like Abram, following wherever the Lord leads, walking in peace and faith, trusting that He will never leave us or forsake us. Even in the silent seasons, He is there. Even when we don't see the next step, He is already making a way. We trust Him as our source and provider, our Lord and our Father.

In this season, God has entrusted us with a vision—one that extends beyond ourselves, beyond our family. He has called us to steward generational wealth, not for personal gain, but for His Kingdom. Pastors and missionaries need resources to carry out the dreams and assignments God has given them. José and I have always carried a heart of generosity, but now, God is teaching us how to give *wisely*, how to steward His blessings with discernment and joy.

We are constantly learning, constantly surrendering, constantly following His lead. And even in this place of discomfort—the stretching, the refining—we live in peace. Because no matter what life looks like, **God is good, and we can trust Him.**

And now, dear reader, I pray for *you*.

I pray that you never allow shame or the lies of the enemy to keep you bound. I pray that you release control to Jesus—the only One who can define your identity, the only One who can restore your purpose, the only One who can remind you of the dreams He placed in your heart. Life with Jesus is the best decision a person can ever make. It isn't always easy. In fact, it rarely is. But with Jesus, you can live in **shalom**—perfect peace, with nothing missing and nothing broken.

We cannot cling to our own understanding. We cannot force our own way.

Give Him the pen.

Let Him rewrite the story of your life into His masterpiece.

We cling to what we know because the unknown is terrifying. It's the monster under the bed—we imagine it, define it, and convince ourselves that if we step into the dark, it will grab us and pull us under. But our imagination is a poor substitute for truth.

And the truth is this: God **only** gives good gifts. He is not waiting to pull you under—He is waiting to lift you up; to rewrite the story you've been trying to control. To take the pages stained with regret, shame, and failure and turn them into something **more than you could ask, think, or imagine**.

I promise you—if you give Him the pen, He will exceed every expectation.

But first, you have to let go.

Find a quiet place. Sit where you won't be disturbed. And **ask God to show you a snapshot of His will for you**. Let that vision fill you with His love. Let it make you brave. And then, when He lays out the path—**refuse to get in your own way**.

He is already writing the masterpiece. Will you let Him finish it?

Appendix
PUTTING FACES
TO NAMES

Meet Jose and me.

My daughter and granddaughter from chapter 12

Jose, me, our kids, with Robin and Tery at our first blended family vacation to Walt Disney World.

www.ingramcontent.com/pod-product-compliance
Lightning Source LLC
Chambersburg PA
CBHW021205130626
46554CB00005B/1991